The Ultimate
Casserole Cookbook

The Ultimate
Casserole Cookbook

175 Great One-Dish Recipes

BARBARA C. JONES

Sterling Publishing Co., Inc.
New York

Art Director: Megan Kirby
Photographer: Evan Bracken, Light Reflections
Food Prep and Styling: David Rowland, Executive Chef, Grove Park Inn Resort and Spa;
Scott Schronce, Executive Sous Chef, Grove Park Inn Resort and Spa
Text: Cookbook Resources, LLC, Barbara Jones and Sheryn Jones

3 5 7 9 10 8 6 4 2

Published by Sterling Publishing Co., Inc.
387 Park Avenue South, New York, NY 10016

Distributed in Canada by Sterling Publishing
Canadian Manda Group, One Atlantic Avenue, Suite 105
Toronto, Ontario, Canada M6K 3E7

Distributed in Australia by Capricorn Link (Australia) Pty Ltd.
P.O. Box 704, Windsor, NSW 2756, Australia

Printed in China

Sterling ISBN 1-4027-0096-2

Table of Contents

Introduction

*T*his cookbook is an eclectic mix of flavors and skill levels. From regional specialties to gourmet delights, the recipes offer delectable taste treats for the simplest and the most educated of human palates. Such a claim can rarely be made and fulfilled, but with the lowly and the grand casserole, it is possible.

The real beginning of the casserole could have started when man began cooking food in pots and combining more than two ingredients. Its roots go back to every generation and every ethnic background. The casserole survives because of its modern adaptations, but still manages to provoke the emotions of comfort, warmth, and security. It survives today as a practical family meal or an elaborate gourmet event. The scope and depth of this simple, yet imperial dish can be found in the pages of The Ultimate Casserole Cookbook.

In its modest beginnings, the casserole referred to a pan or pot with a lid in which food was cooked. When several ingredients were cooked in the casserole pot or pan, the food itself became known as a casserole. And so today, the word "casserole" means both the container and the food contained therein.

Casserole containers themselves started out as large, heavy iron pots with lids, handles, and feet for cooking on open fires. Lids kept the heat in and provided a moist cooking method that made even the poorest cuts of meat tender if cooked long enough. To this day, characteristics such as lids and handles have survived because of the practical nature of the casserole itself. The idea of serving food in the same container in which the food was cooked has led to elaborate containers and elaborate food combinations.

Casserole containers come in many sizes, shapes, and materials. The Dutch oven is the oldest of containers to survive. It's a large kettle or pot, favored in cast iron, usually with an opening larger than its base with a tight fitting lid and handles.

Today's casserole dishes are round, oval, square, and rectangular, and they're able to hold varying amounts. They can be shallow or deep or any depth in between. They can be made of copper, cast iron, enameled iron, stainless steel, aluminum, ceramic, or glass. Their size, shape, and material become the cook's choice just as the foods prepared in them.

The casserole's convenience, practicality, elegance, and its simplicity all work to give us one of the most popular and most versatile of all food combinations…and it even comes with its own container!

Enjoy and celebrate!

Casserole Basics

*C*asseroles can generally be defined as a one-dish meal combining more than two or three ingredients, cooked in the oven, and served in the same dish in which it is cooked. They can be baked in containers in a wide variety of sizes, shapes, and materials.

Basic Pan Materials

When choosing "casseroles" or baking dishes, the heaviest is usually the best. The heaviest-gauge pans spread and hold the heat evenly, thereby cooking the contents evenly. They also will last longer and have a tendency not to warp. Also, lids with casseroles are very helpful. Glass casseroles or baking dishes may be covered with aluminum foil for the oven and plastic wrap for the refrigerator, but lids are preferable with other materials. Listed below are materials, sizes, and shapes for various casseroles, baking dishes, and pans. Beyond the basics mentioned, personal preference based on looks and how you plan to use the pans will guide your buying decisions.

Cast iron

Some cooks believe a cast-iron skillet is a must in the kitchen to get the "old fashioned" flavors they remember from mother or grandmother. Cast iron is a very good material for cooking because it cooks evenly and it can go from the stovetop to the oven. The problem comes when you move it from the stovetop to the oven and then take it out of the oven because it can be very heavy. That may not seem like much of a problem, but wait until you have a cast-iron pot, skillet, or saute pan full of steaming, hot food and you're gripping it with two hands, carrying it from one place to another. That's when reality sets in and "heavy" takes on a new meaning.

Copper

Copper is the chef's delight and usually left to the professionals because of the expense. Besides looking great and cooking evenly, it's undeniably the best type of pan. It's great if you can afford them.

Coated Aluminum

Heavy-duty aluminum with non-stick coatings (which eventually do wear out regardless the manufacturer's claims) are very popular because they are reasonably priced, lighter weight, and cook evenly. Those that are anodized are stronger and will probably last longer.

Stainless Steel

Stainless steel is one step up from anodized aluminum in the looks department. If anodized aluminum or heavy-duty aluminum with non-stick surfaces isn't good-looking enough for you and copper is out of your price range, check out stainless steel. All good stainless steel pans have a layer of copper or aluminum on the bottom and sides or a layer sandwiched between the coatings of stainless steel. Make sure they are heavy and not light weight.

Enameled iron

Enameled iron puts a pretty face on a plain pan. The more expensive ones have the qualities needed for cooking, but also the outside attractiveness needed for the dinner table. Don't let the outside distract you from the material properties, however. When your casserole dish is sitting on the table looking great for honored dinner guests, you want its contents to taste as good as the pan looks.

Ceramic

Ceramic- or porcelain-coated metal falls into the same category as enameled iron. It was created for its attractiveness at the table. Just make sure the metal properties meet your needs.

Glass

Glass pans are probably the most inexpensive and most widely used. It's the dish you use for most family meals. It's also the dish you take to covered dish suppers. If it gets broken or lost during the clean up, you won't be devastated. You'll just go buy another one, tape your name to the bottom, and take it to the next covered dish supper.

Pan Sizes

If you could only choose three sizes, you might consider the 8 -x 12-inch rectangular pan, the 9- x 13-inch rectangular pan and the 9-inch square pan. If you could just have one, the 9- x 13-inch would have to be the first choice. Its general all-purpose size and shape holds most of the casseroles found in this book. But don't take our word for it, shop and check out all the sizes and shapes. You won't believe the variety.

Casserole Containers
7 x 11 x 2 yields 6 to 8 cups
9 x 9 x 2 yields 10 cups
9 x 13 x 2 yields 15 cups

Sauce Pans

Small: 1 to 2 cups
Medium: 6 cups (1½ quarts, 1.1 L)
Large: 16 cups (4 quarts, 4.4 L)
Note: It's important for all pots and pans to have lids.

Pasta Pans

4- to 8-quart (4.4 to 8.8 L) pot large enough for 1 to 2 pounds (454 to 908 g) of pasta and its equivalent water.

Basic Pasta Styles

Tube–Shaped Pastas

Cappelletti: hat shaped stuffed pastas, similar to ravioli
Elbow pasta: any variety of curved, tubular pastas
Macaroni: tube shapes of different lengths about ½ inch (12 mm) wide
Manicotti: large tubes used for filling
Mostaccioli: tubes with straight or rippled edges
Penne: diagonally cut tubes
Ravioli: square shaped with filling
Rigatoni: large grooved macaroni
Tortellini: similar to cappelletti; small stuffed pasta
Tortelloni: large tortellini
Ziti: thin tubes available in varying lengths

Ribbon–Shaped Pastas

Bavettine, Bavette: narrow ribbons
Fettuccine, Fettucini: thin, flat egg noodles about ¼ inch (6 mm) wide
Linguine: narrow, flat noodles about ⅛ inch (3 mm) wide
Margherite: flat, narrow noodles with rippled edges
Pappardelle: long, flat noodles about ½ inch (12 mm) wide with rippled edges
Tagliarin: long, paper-thin ribbons

Strands

Bucatini, Bucatoni: hollow, long strands
Capelli d'angelo: also known as angel hair pasta; long, extremely fine, delicate strands
Capellini: slightly thicker than capelli d'angelo
Fedelini: very fine spaghetti
Fidellini: another name for capellini
Lasagna: long noodles about 2 to 3 inches (5 to 7.5 cm) wide
Spaghettini: very thin spaghetti, but thicker than fettuccine
Vermicelli: very long, thin strands

Spirals

Cavatappi: also known as "corkscrew" pasta; short, thin spirals
Fusilli: also known as "little springs;" spirals about 1½ inches (3.5 cm) long
Rotini: small spirals

Shells

Conchiglie: also known as "conch shells"
Conchiglioni: larger version of conchiglie
Gnocchi: small, ripple-edged shells
Maruzze: seashells in all sizes

Patterns

Farfalle: bow-tie or butterfly shaped pasta
Farfallini: small version of farfalle
Rotelle: small, spoked-wheels

Freezing Casseroles

Baking and freezing casseroles can be great way to save time and money. For best success, follow the guidelines below.

1. Cook casserole as directed, but reduce cooking by 10 to 15 minutes so it won't overcook when it's reheated.

2. Always cover casserole or baking dishes tightly before freezing.

3. Use an oven-to-freezer container so you don't have to disturb the dish before freezing.

4. Reduce the amounts of seasonings used because they may intensify with time.

5. Let casserole cool before freezing.

6. Store in freezer no more than 2 to 4 weeks.

7. Defrost food in refrigerator.

Brunch Casseroles

*B*runch days are special, no doubt about it. They're the days when you don't have to rush off to work or the days when you want to treat company to a good morning treat. The brunch recipes in this chapter combine fruits, meats, eggs and more in a variety of creative traditional – and new – ways. For a savory start to one of your special days, consider the Apple-Sausage Breakfast Casserole on page 17, the Creamy Brunch Casserole on page 20, or the Cheesy Zucchini Frittata on page 25.

Spinach Quiche

10-ounce (283 g) package frozen chopped spinach

9-inch (23 cm) pastry shell

¼ cup (20 g) grated parmesan cheese

3 eggs, beaten

1½ cups (337 g) cottage cheese, drained

1 cup (240 mL) whipping cream

2 tablespoons minced onion

1½ teaspoons salt

½ teaspoon pepper

1 teaspoon caraway seeds

¼ teaspoon nutmeg

½ teaspoon worcestershire

3 drops Tabasco

3 tablespoons butter, melted

This is a great dish to serve at a luncheon. You will want to make this quiche lots of times, so invest in a metal quiche pan that has a removable bottom.

Cook spinach according to package directions and drain thoroughly. Line the pie pan with pastry and bake at 400° (200° C) for 8 minutes. Cool. Reduce oven temperature to 350° (175° C).

Sprinkle parmesan cheese in bottom of shell. Combine all remaining ingredients except butter. Pour butter over cheese. Melt butter and pour over top.

Bake for 30 to 45 minutes or until toothpick comes out clean.

Good Morning Sausage

1 pound (453 g) pork sausage

6 eggs, beaten

2 cups (480 mL) milk

6 slices bread, cubed

1 teaspoon dry mustard

1 teaspoon salt

1 cup (110 g) grated cheddar cheese

⅛ teaspoon oregano

This casserole calls for hot biscuits and straw-berry preserves.

In skillet, brown sausage and drain. Mix all ingredients together. Place in a sprayed 9- x 13-inch (23 x 33 cm) casserole dish.

Cover and refrigerate for several hours or overnight. Bake at 350° (175° C) for 45 minutes or until mixture is brown around edges.

Egg McMaster

24 eggs

½ cup (120 mL) milk

⅓ cup (80 g) butter

½ cup (120 mL) sherry

3 4-ounce (113 g) cans mushrooms, drained

1 red bell pepper, chopped

2 10-ounce (283 g) cans cream of mushroom soup

¼ teaspoon salt

2 cups (220 g) grated cheddar cheese

The red bell pepper adds a good flavor to these eggs and also makes an attractive, colorful dish! Leftovers can be warmed the next day.

Beat eggs and milk to scramble. Melt butter in skillet. Add eggs and lightly scramble. Pour into sprayed 9- x 13-inch (23 x 33) baking dish.

In a separate bowl, mix together sherry, mushrooms, bell pepper, soup, and salt. Pour over eggs and sprinkle cheese over mixture. Refrigerate covered for 10 to 12 hours. Bake at 350° (175° C) for 20 to 25 minutes.

Quick Brunch Bake

1 cup (90 g) seasoned breadcrumbs,
    divided

2 10-ounce (283 g) packages frozen
    chopped spinach, thawed

24-ounce (680 g) carton small curd cottage
    cheese

¾ cup (60 g) grated parmesan cheese

5 eggs, divided

A touch of nutmeg enhances the aroma and flavor of spinach; so for that special touch, sprinkle a little nutmeg over this casserole just before serving.

Grease or spray an 8- x 8-inch (20 cm) baking dish and spread a fourth of the breadcrumbs over bottom. Bake at 350° (175° C) for 5 minutes or until slightly brown.

Drain spinach by rolling in paper towels and squeezing until thoroughly drained. Mix spinach with cottage cheese, parmesan, and 3 beaten eggs and spread over breadcrumbs.

Beat remaining eggs and pour over mixture. Bake covered at 350° (175° C) for 40 to 45 minutes or until a fork inserted in center comes out clean. Let cool slightly to make slicing easier.

Apple-Sausage Breakfast Casserole

2 pounds (907 g) ground pork sausage

8 slices bread

1½ cups (265 g) sliced apples

⅔ teaspoons dry mustard

8 eggs, lightly beaten

1½ cups (165 g) grated sharp cheddar
  cheese

3 cups (720 mL) milk

Because this casserole needs to sit overnight before baking, you can sleep in and have a fabulous breakfast, too. Before cooking in the morning, let casserole stand out of refrigerator for 20 to 25 minutes and cook an extra 5 minutes. Delicious served with hot biscuits!

In a large skillet, fry the sausage, breaking into small bits as it cooks. Drain on paper towels, reserving some of the fat. Lightly grease a 9- x 13-inch (23 x 33 cm) baking dish. Place the sausage in the baking dish.

Remove the crust from the bread and tear into small pieces or cut into cubes. Saute the apples in the sausage fat. In a large bowl combine the apples, bread, mustard, eggs, cheese, and milk until well mixed.

Pour apple mixture over the sausage. Cover with foil and refrigerate overnight. In the morning bake covered at 350° (175° C) for 30 minutes. Remove the foil and bake uncovered for an additional 30 minutes.

Southern Cheese Grits

1½ cups (360 mL) milk

3½ cups (840 mL) water

½ teaspoon salt

1¼ cup (190 g) quick grits

½ cup (115 g) butter

6-ounce (170 g) roll garlic cheese

3 cups (330 g) shredded cheddar or colby cheese

½ teaspoon cayenne

½ teaspoon garlic salt

1 tablespoon worcestershire sauce

Paprika

You haven't had breakfast in New Orleans if you haven't had "grits" served with your eggs!

Boil milk, water, and salt in medium saucepan. Add grits and stir to mix. Reduce heat and cook until desired doneness. (Make sure heat is low enough so grits won't stick to bottom of pan.) Stir several times.

Add butter and cheeses and stir to melt. Add cayenne, garlic salt, and worcestershire sauce. Stir well.

Pour into sprayed 3-quart (3 L) casserole and sprinkle with paprika. Bake covered at 350° (175° C) for 15 to 20 minutes or until thoroughly heated.

Brunch Casserole

6-ounce (170 g) box seasoned croutons

1 cup (110 g) grated Swiss cheese

1 cup (110 g) grated cheddar cheese

1½ cups (165 g) grated Monterey Jack cheese

1 pound (453 g) bacon, cooked and crumbled

1 pint (500 mL) half-and-half cream

10 eggs

½ cup (120 mL) milk

¾ teaspoon salt

¾ teaspoon white pepper

The depth of baking pans can vary, so make sure your baking pan is fairly dee for this dish. This recipe makes enough for the whole gang!

Spread croutons on bottom of sprayed 9- x 13-inch (23 x 33 cm) baking dish. Sprinkle cheeses on top of croutons. Add bacon on top of cheese.

In mixing bowl, combine cream, eggs, milk, salt, and white pepper; mix well. Pour over bacon.

Cover and refrigerate several hours. Uncover and bake at 350° (175° C) for 30 to 45 minutes or until bubbly.

Creamy Brunch Casserole

4 slices bacon, chopped

½ pound (226 g) dried beef, chopped

½ cup (115 g) butter, divided

½ pound (226 g) fresh mushrooms, sliced

½ cup (70 g) flour

1 quart (1 L) milk

16 eggs

¼ teaspoon salt

Pepper

This recipe calls for the eggs to be scrambled just until very soft. Do not overcook the eggs!

Brown bacon to crispy in skillet. Remove from pan and drain. Add beef, half the butter, and mushrooms.

Saute lightly. Sprinkle flour over mixture. Cook 3 minutes. Gradually stir in milk. Cook until sauce is thickened and smooth, stirring constantly. Set aside.

Combine eggs, salt, and pepper in bowl and scramble eggs in remaining butter in skillet until very soft. In a 9- x 13-inch (23 x 33 cm) casserole, alternate layers of scrambled eggs and sauce.

Top with crumbled bacon. Bake at 275° (135° C) for 30 minutes.

Mexican Quiche

1½ (680 g) pounds ground beef

1 envelope taco seasoning mix

10-inch (25 cm) deep-dish pie shell, baked

2 cups (220 g) grated Monterey Jack cheese, divided

2 cups (220 g) grated cheddar cheese, divided

4 eggs, lightly beaten

1 cup (240 mL) milk

Salsa

Change up your Mexican supper; forget the enchiladas and serve quesadillas plus some guacamole and chips.

Brown ground beef until crumbly, then drain. Mix in taco seasoning and stir. In baked pie shell, sprinkle half the cheeses over bottom of pie shell.

Spoon in beef mixture evenly and sprinkle remaining cheeses on top. Pour mixture of eggs and milk on top.

Bake at 350° (175° C) for 30 to 45 minutes or until golden brown. Serve with salsa on the side.

Bacon-Spinach Quiche

2 9-inch (23 cm) deep dish, unbaked pie shells

3 tablespoons butter, softened

2 10-ounce (567 g) packages frozen chopped spinach, thawed

1 pound (453 g) bacon, cooked

2 cups (480 mL) whipping cream

8 eggs, beaten

⅔ cup (70 g) shredded Swiss cheese

¾ teaspoon salt

⅛ teaspoon ground nutmeg

This quiche is not only great for a brunch, it is great for lunch.

Prepare pie shells by rubbing butter on inside bottom and sides of deep dish. Drain spinach by putting between several layers of paper towels and squeezing liquid out.

Layer spinach in both pie shells and crumble cooked bacon on top. Whisk together cream, eggs, cheese, and seasonings, and pour over spinach and bacon. Bake at 425° (220° C) for 10 minutes. Reduce heat to 325° (160° C) and bake 35 to 40 minutes longer.

Eggs Mornay

12 eggs

3 cups (729 mL) milk, divided

½ cup (115 g) melted butter

1½ teaspoon salt

½ teaspoon white pepper

¼ teaspoon cayenne

½ cup (70 g) flour

½ cup (55 g) grated Swiss cheese

¼ cup (20 g) parmesan cheese, divided

½ pound (226 g) fresh mushrooms, minced

6 tablespoons melted butter, divided

3 tablespoons snipped parsley

½ tablespoon snipped tarragon leaves

1 cup (90 g) seasoned breadcrumbs

Roma tomatoes, sliced

Dare to be different; forget the quiche and serve Eggs Mornay for lunch or supper. You will have rave reviews!

Carefully place eggs in boiling water and cook until hard-boiled, about 12 to 15 minutes. Remove from heat, drain and let cool.

Heat milk in large saucepan over low heat until steaming. Pour 2 cups hot milk into blender and set aside remaining hot milk. To blender add ½ cup butter, salt, white pepper, cayenne, and flour, and blend for 30 seconds.

Pour blender mixture into saucepan with remaining milk and cook over low heat, stirring constantly, until thickened, about 2 to 3 minutes. Add Swiss cheese and half the parmesan cheese to milk and stir until cheese has melted. Remove from heat, cover and set aside.

Peel shells from eggs and cut lengthwise in half. Separate yolk from whites and set aside. In skillet, saute mushrooms in 4 tablespoons butter until tender and translucent. Stir in parsley and tarragon.

In a separate bowl, mash egg yolks and stir in ½ cup milk-cheese sauce and sauteed mushrooms. Scoop yolk mixture into whites of eggs and set aside.

In a sprayed 9- x 13-inch (23 x 33 cm) baking dish, pour a thin layer of milk-cheese sauce over bottom. Place eggs in baking dish with filling side up. Pour over remaining milk-cheese sauce.

Toss breadcrumbs with remaining butter and remaining parmesan cheese and sprinkle over eggs. Cover with foil and bake at 350° (175° C) for 25 to 30 minutes. Serve over toast points with fresh sliced tomatoes to the side.

Mexican Brunch

10½-ounce (273 g) can mushroom soup

4-ounce (113 g) can chopped green chilies, drained

7-ounce (198 g) can green chili salsa

1 cup (240 g) sour cream

½ teaspoon coriander

½ teaspoon ground cumin

1-pound (453 g) package hot ground pork sausage

4 tablespoons butter

7 eggs, beaten

½ cup (120 g) small curd cottage cheese, drained

½ cup (75 g) chopped green onion tops

8 12-inch (30 cm) flour tortillas, buttered

1½ cup (165 g) grated cheddar cheese

1 cup (110 g) grated Monterey Jack cheese

This is a meal in itself — you don't need biscuits or toast. Serve with fruit to add a light touch to this spicy casserole.

In a mixing bowl, whisk together mushroom soup, green chilies, salsa, sour cream, coriander, and cumin; set aside. Brown sausage and cook until crumbled. Drain thoroughly; set aside.

In skillet over low heat, melt butter, scramble eggs lightly, and stir in cottage cheese and green onions. Add 3 tablespoons of mushroom-green chili sauce and all the crumbled sausage. Mix thoroughly until set and remove from heat.

Spread a small amount of sauce over bottom of sprayed 9- x 13-inch (23 x 33 cm) baking dish. Spoon egg-sausage mixture into eight flour tortillas and roll tortillas up. Place in baking dish with seam side down. Arrange tortillas in baking dish and cover with remaining sauce.

Sprinkle cheddar cheese and Monterey Jack cheese over top of sauce. Bake at 350° (175° C) for 25 to 30 minutes or until cheeses are bubbly.

Cheesy Zucchini Frittata

4 eggs

4 cups (700 g) shredded zucchini

2 cups (900 g) peeled, shredded carrots

½ cup (70 g) flour

¾ cup (180 g) mayonnaise

1 cup (110 g) shredded Monterey Jack cheese

½ cup (40 g) grated parmesan cheese

¼ cup (40 g) chopped onion

1 teaspoon basil

Pepper to taste

Although frittatas are famous for their savory herbs and spices, the zucchini and carrots in this recipe add a flavor of their own.

In mixing bowl beat eggs. Fold in zucchini, carrots, flour, mayonnaise, cheeses, onion, basil, and pepper.

Pour into a buttered quiche pan and bake at 375° (190° C) for 30 minutes or until set.

Baked Potatoes Sunrise

4 Idaho baking potatoes

Olive oil or butter

½ pound (226 g) hot, ground pork sausage

1 cup (150 g) chopped green onion with tops, divided

¼ cup (45 g) minced red bell pepper

¼ cup (60 mL) whipping cream

3 egg yolks

¼ cup (60 g) sour cream

1 teaspoon salt

½ teaspoon white pepper

Hungarian paprika

Fresh parsley

Fresh tomato slices

Perk up any meal with these "twice baked" potatoes! (To speed up the cooking process, push metal skewers through center to conduct heat.)

Wash potatoes and stick skin several times with fork. Rub skin with a little oil or butter and arrange on baking sheet. Bake at 350° (175° C) for 1 hour 30 minutes or until potatoes are soft on the inside. Remove potatoes from oven to cool.

Brown sausage in skillet until crumbly and cooked through. Drain sausage on paper towels and transfer to large mixing bowl. Add a little oil to skillet and saute ¾ cup green onion and red bell pepper until tender and translucent. Add onion and bell pepper to sausage in mixing bowl.

When potatoes are cool enough to touch, cut small oval in outer skin on top of potato. With a small spoon, scoop out pulp being careful to leave shell in tact. Leave about ¼-inch (6 mm) thickness inside outer skin.

Put potato pulp in a separate bowl and mash with a fork or potato masher. Slowly stir in whipping cream, egg yolks, sour cream, salt, and white pepper. Stir well to mix ingredients and to make a creamy texture. Add a little more cream if mixture seems too dry.

Slowly fold in sausage-onion mixture and stir to combine. Spoon this filling into individual potato shells allowing filling to rise above top of potato skin. Place stuffed potatoes back on baking sheet and sprinkle top of each potato with paprika.

Bake at 350° (175° C) for 10 to 15 minutes to heat thoroughly. Remove from oven and garnish with parsley and remaining minced green onion tops. Serve with tomato slices on the side.

Yellow Squash-Sausage Mix

2 pounds (907 g) yellow squash, cut into
   bite-size pieces

¼ cup (35 g) chopped onion

1 pound (453 g) Italian sausage

½ cup (85 g) fine cracker crumbs

2 eggs, beaten

½ cup (40 g) grated parmesan cheese,
   divided

¼ teaspoon thyme

¼ teaspoon rosemary

¼ teaspoon garlic powder

Salt and pepper to taste

*Summer gardens produce the most beautiful
squash! When buying yellow squash, choose
the smallest ones since they have fewer seeds.*

Cook squash in boiling, salted water until tender;
drain. In skillet, brown onion and sausage; drain.

Add squash and remaining ingredients, except 2
tablespoons parmesan cheese; mixing well.

Divide mixture between 2 8-inch (20 cm) pie plates.
Sprinkle with remaining parmesan cheese. Bake at
350° (175° C) for 45 minutes, or until brown.

Brunch Broccoli Squares

¾ cup (112 g) chopped onion

2 tablespoons butter

2 10-ounce (283 g) packages frozen, chopped broccoli, thawed

12-ounce (340 g) package shredded cheddar cheese, divided

1⅓ cups (320 mL) half-and-half cream

4 eggs

¾ cup (112 g) buttermilk baking mix

½ teaspoon white pepper

This unique casserole is served by cutting it in squares. For a lovely table presentation, consider arranging the squares on a bed of chopped spinach and garnish with fresh tomato slices.

Saute onion in butter until tender. Pat broccoli with several paper towels to make sure all liquid is drained. Combine onion, broccoli, and 2 cups (200 g) cheese; mix well.

Spread mixture in a buttered 7- x 11-inch (18 x 28 cm) baking dish. In a bowl, combine and beat together the cream, eggs, baking mix, and pepper; mix until mixture is fairly smooth. Pour over broccoli mixture.

Bake uncovered at 375° (190° C) for 30 minutes or until set in middle of casserole. Remove from oven and sprinkle remaining cheese over casserole.

Return to oven for about 3 or 4 minutes. Cut into squares to serve. Mozzarella cheese may be substituted for the cheddar cheese.

Sausage and Chile Bake

7-ounce (198 g) can whole green chiles

1 pound (453 g) hot sausage, cooked, crumbled

2 tablespoons minced, dried onion flakes

5 eggs, lightly beaten

1 pint (480 mL) half-and-half cream

⅔ cup (66 g) shredded parmesan cheese

½ cup (50 g) grated Swiss cheese

½ teaspoon seasoned salt

This breakfast casserole can be made the night before and refrigerated. Allow an extra 5 minutes of baking time.

Butter a 9- x 13-inch (23 x 33 cm) baking dish and line the bottom with split and seeded green chiles. Sprinkle sausage over chiles.

In a medium-size bowl, combine onion flakes, eggs, cream, cheeses, and seasoned salt. Pour over the sausage and bake uncovered at 350° (175° C) for 35 minutes or until top is lightly browned.

Allow to set for 5 to 10 minutes before slicing and serving.

Breakfast Potatoes

9-inch (23 cm) unbaked pie shell

1 pound (453 g) mild or hot sausage

16-ounce (453 g) carton small curd cottage cheese

3 eggs

2½ cups (562 g) well seasoned warm, mashed potatoes

⅔ cup (160 g) sour cream

¼ stick (30 g) margarine, melted

1 teaspoon dried oregano

¼ teaspoon garlic powder

½ teaspoon seasoned salt

⅛ teaspoon cayenne pepper

2¼ cups (225 g) shredded cheddar cheese

Salsa

This is a hardy start for the day! And a lot healthier than "hash browns." Serve with some fresh fruit and a buttered hot biscuit.

In a 375° (190° C) oven, bake pie shell for 7 minutes. Set aside.

Crumble the sausage into skillet and cook thoroughly; drain well. Place the cottage cheese and eggs in a processor container. Process until well blended.

Pour into a large bowl; add the potatoes, sour cream, margarine, and seasonings, mixing well. Spoon the sausage into the pie shell. Sprinkle with cheese.

Bake uncovered at 350° (175° C) for about 55 minutes. To serve, cut in pie wedge shapes and serve with salsa.

Rice & Pasta Casseroles

*R*ice and pasta casseroles are some of the best comfort foods imaginable. They also offer lots of room for creative recipe changes. The Exceptional Tetrazzini on page 34, for example, can be made with chicken or turkey, while the Cheesy Spinach Manicotti on page 38 works just as well with lasagna. If you cook you're way through this chapter, you'll soon be an expert on the incredible range of pastas and rices available.

Italian Manicotti

1 pound (453 g) lean ground round

3 cloves garlic, minced

2 onions, chopped

28-ounce (793 g) can diced tomatoes, undrained

8-ounce (226 g) package fresh mushrooms, sliced

1 teaspoon fennel seed

2 teaspoons basil

1 teaspoon seasoned salt

½ teaspoon pepper

2 10-ounce (283 g) packages frozen chopped spinach, thawed and well drained

½ cup (40 g) parmesan cheese, divided

2 cups (480 g) small curd cottage cheese, drained

¼ teaspoon nutmeg

½ teaspoon pepper

14 manicotti shells, cooked al dente

Manicotti is a little more trouble than some dishes, but it is well worth the effort and leftovers freeze well.

In a large skillet, brown ground beef, then add garlic and onion, and reduce heat to low. Simmer for 10 minutes and drain. Add tomatoes and liquid, mushrooms, fennel seed, basil, salt, and pepper and stir to mix. Bring to a boil, reduce heat and simmer for 10 minutes; stir occasionally.

In a separate bowl, stir together spinach, half the parmesan, cottage cheese, nutmeg, and pepper. In a sprayed 9- x 13-inch (23 x 33 cm) baking dish, spoon about one-third of beef sauce evenly over bottom of dish.

Fill uncooked manicotti shells with spinach mixture and place on beef layer in baking dish. Repeat until all spinach mixture has been used in manicotti shells.

Pour remaining beef sauce evenly over manicotti shells to cover. Sprinkle remaining parmesan cheese over top. Cover and bake at 350° (175° C) for 1 hour 30 minutes or until shells are tender.

Exceptional Tetrazzini

1 cup (73 g) fresh mushrooms, halved

⅓ cup (80 g) butter

2 tablespoons flour

14-ounce (420 mL) can chicken broth

¼ cup (60 mL) dry vermouth

⅔ cup (158 mL) whipping cream

3 cooked chicken breasts, chopped

⅛ teaspoon nutmeg

½ teaspoon seasoned salt

4 ounces (113 g) uncooked angel hair pasta

3 tablespoons olive oil

½ teaspoon white pepper

⅓ cup (27 g) grated parmesan cheese

Tetrazzini is generally made with leftover chicken — turkey works well too. Good family food!

In a skillet saute the mushrooms in the butter. Remove mushrooms leaving melted butter in skillet. Sprinkle flour over butter; cook on low heat for 2 minutes, stirring constantly.

Gradually stir in chicken broth; simmer, while stirring until thickened and smooth. Remove from heat and add vermouth, cream, chicken, mushrooms, and seasonings.

Cook the pasta according to package directions; drain. In a large bowl, combine the pasta and chicken mixture, mixing gently. Spoon into a buttered 3-quart (3 L) baking dish. Sprinkle with cheese. Bake at 350° (175° C) for 30 minutes.

Zucchini Fettuccini

12-ounce (340 g) package fettuccini

8-ounce (240 mL) carton whipping cream, divided

8 ounces (226 g) fresh mushrooms, sliced

1 stick (120 g) butter, half sliced

3 to 4 zucchini, cut into 2½-inch (6 cm) strips

⅓ cup (9 g) grated parmesan cheese

⅓ cup chopped fresh parsley

½ teaspoon seasoned salt

¼ teaspoon white pepper

This vegetarian dish features a rich sauces and delicate vegetables. Garnish with hot pepper flakes if you prefer a spicier flavor.

Cook fettuccini as directed on package; drain. Toss with ¼ cup cream. Saute mushrooms in ½ stick butter. Add zucchini, remaining cream and sliced butter.

Heat, cover and simmer for about 3 minutes. Add cooked pasta to mushroom-zucchini mixture. Toss with parmesan cheese and parsley; mix well.

Spoon into a buttered 3-quart (3 L) baking dish. Heat at 325° (165° C) for about 10 minutes.

Italian Dinner

2 pounds (907 g) lean ground round beef

1 onion, chopped

1 sweet red bell pepper, chopped

2 ribs celery, chopped

2 garlic cloves, finely minced

32-ounce (907 g) jar spaghetti sauce

3 6-ounce (170 g) jars sliced mushrooms, drained

¾ teaspoon ground oregano

½ teaspoon Italian seasoning

Salt and pepper to taste

8-ounce (226 g) package medium egg noodles

8-ounce (226 g) package cream cheese, softened

1 pint (480 g) carton sour cream

1 cup (100 g) grated parmesan cheese

16-ounce (453 g) package shredded mozzarella cheese

Baked Italian dishes are famous for their rich flavorful sauces, bursting with herbal flavor. This recipe tastes wonderful on the first night, and even better as leftovers.

In a very large skillet, brown beef, onion, bell pepper, celery, and garlic; drain. Add the spaghetti sauce, mushrooms, and seasonings. Heat to boiling, turn heat down, and simmer for about 15 minutes.

Cook noodles according to package directions; drain. With mixer or hand mixer, beat cream cheese until creamy; add sour cream and cheeses.

Butter a deep 9- x 13-inch (23 x 33 cm) baking dish. Layer half the noodles, beef mixture and cheeses. Repeat layers.

Bake covered at 325° (165° C) for 30 minutes; remove covering and bake another 10 to 15 minutes.

Three-Cheese Fusilli Bake

1 tablespoon salt

1 tablespoon olive oil

1 pound (453 g) spinach fusilli

1 cup (240 mL) whipping cream

½ cup (120 mL) dry white wine

½ teaspoon Tabasco

1½ cups (165 g) blue cheese

1 cup (110 g) brie cheese, rind removed, cubed

3 cups (330 g) grated cheddar cheese, divided

1 tablespoon dried thyme

2 tablespoons sage

1 to 2 tablespoons ground white pepper to taste

4 to 5 roma tomatoes, peeled, thinly sliced

3 tablespoons grated parmesan cheese

2 tablespoons snipped fresh basil

If you don't have a soufflé dish, a deep, round casserole dish will work fine.

Fill a large pot three-quarters full of water and bring to a boil. Add 1 tablespoon salt, 1 tablespoon oil, and fusilli, and cook until fusilli is al dente. Drain and rinse under cold water. Repeat process and set aside.

In heavy saucepan, slowly heat to simmering whipping cream, wine, and Tabasco, stirring constantly. Gradually add all cheeses, except 1 cup cheddar, a little at a time as they melt. Whisk or stir constantly as cheese melts and be sure not to let milk scorch or burn on bottom of saucepan.

When cheeses have melted and mixture is smooth and creamy, whisk in thyme, sage and white pepper. Remove from heat and continue stirring for 3 to 5 minutes as cheese mixture cools.

In a sprayed 2½-quart (2.5 L) souffle dish, arrange one-third of the cheese mixture over the fusilli and sprinkle one-third of the remaining grated cheddar cheese. Repeat process in two more layers, ending with grated cheddar on top.

Carefully put souffle dish in oven and bake at 350° (175° C) for 15 to 20 minutes. Remove from oven and cover with aluminum foil and bake another 15 minutes.

Remove from oven and uncover. Place tomato slices over the top in nice overlapping design and sprinkle parmesan on top. Bake at 350° (175° C) for another 10 minutes uncovered. Remove from oven and sprinkle with fresh basil and serve.

Zesty Vegetable Lasagna

14½-ounce (411 g) can Italian-style stewed tomatoes

1⅔ cups (400 mL) pasta sauce

2 cups (480 g) non-fat cottage cheese

¾ cup (60 g) grated parmesan cheese

¼ teaspoon salt

¼ teaspoon white pepper

9 lasagna noodles, uncooked, divided

4 zucchini, shredded, divided

7 1-ounce (28 g) provolone cheese slices, cut into strips, divided

The only reason you need a head start on this delicious lasagna is because it needs to chill for 8 hours — but it is so easy to "put together" because you do not have to cook the lasagna noodles. It's worth the 8-hour wait.

Stir together stewed tomatoes and pasta sauce. Set aside. Stir together cottage cheese, parmesan cheese, salt, and white pepper.

Spoon one-third of tomato mixture into sprayed 9-x13- inch (23 x 33 cm) baking dish. Place 3 uncooked lasagna noodles over tomato mixture and top with one third of grated zucchini. Spoon one-third of cheese mixture over zucchini and top with one-third of provolone cheese strips.

Repeat layering procedure twice. Cover and chill at least 8 hours. Remove from refrigerator and let stand for 30 minutes. Bake covered at 350° (175° C) for 45 minutes. Uncover and bake additional 20 minutes. Let rest 15 minutes before serving.

Cheesy Spinach Manicotti

1 large onion, chopped

½ cup (85 g) chopped green, bell pepper

2 garlic cloves, finely chopped

1 tablespoon oil

16-ounce (453 g) carton ricotta cheese

1½ cups (165 g) shredded mozzarella cheese, divided

3-ounce (85 g) package cream cheese, softened

½ cup (40 g) grated parmesan cheese, divided

1 tablespoon Italian seasoning

½ teaspoon seasoned salt

This cheese-lovers manicotti! is a great dish for family or company. Add a green salad with an Italian dressing and you have dinner!

In a skillet, saute the onion, bell pepper, and garlic in the oil; set aside. In mixing bowl, combine the ricotta, ¾ cup mozzarella, cream cheese, half the parmesan cheese, and the seasonings; beat until smooth.

Drain the spinach well by squeezing between paper towels. Combine onion mixture with the spinach, mixing well. Spoon mixture into cooked manicotti shells.

Pour half the spaghetti sauce into a well greased 9- x 13-inch (23 x 33 cm) baking dish. Arrange shells over spaghetti sauce, then pour remaining sauce over the

½ teaspoon black pepper

10-ounce (283 g) package frozen chopped
spinach, thawed

8 manicotti shells, cooked, drained

26-ounce (737 g) jar spaghetti sauce

top of manicotti shells. Bake covered at 350° (175° C)
for 30 minutes.

Uncover and sprinkle remaining mozzarella cheese
and parmesan cheese over top. Bake another 5 minutes until cheese has melted. Serve immediately.

Spinach-Baked Penne

12- to 14-ounce (340 to 396 g) package
ground hot Italian sausage

4 cloves garlic, minced

2 onions, chopped

28-ounce (793 g) can crushed tomatoes,
undrained

½ cup (120 g) pesto sauce

½ teaspoon salt

¼ teaspoon pepper

10-ounce (283 g) package penne or ziti

10-ounce (283 g) package fresh spinach
leaves, torn

2 cups (226 g) shredded mozzarella cheese

1 cup (85 g) grated fresh parmesan cheese,
divided

*This dish is easy to put together and extra easy
to eat!*

In large skillet, brown sausage. Push sausage to one
side in skillet, add garlic and onion and cook a minute
or two. Stir ingredients together, crumble sausage
and cook on low until sausage is no longer pink and
cooked throughout.

Drain sausage and pour in tomatoes and liquid. Cook
on low for 10 minutes or until liquid begins to thicken
into a sauce, stirring occasionally. Add pesto, salt and
pepper and stir to mix well.

In large pot, add 2 to 3 times more water than penne
or ziti and bring to a boil. Add salt and pasta and cook
until al dente. Drain pasta thoroughly and pour into a
large bowl.

Add spinach, mozzarella and half the parmesan to the
pasta and stir to mix. Add tomato mixture and stir. In
a sprayed 9- x 13-inch (23 x 33 cm) baking dish, pour
all ingredients and spread evenly in dish.

Sprinkle remaining parmesan cheese over top of
dish. Bake at 350° (175° C) for 30 to 35 minutes or
until bubbly.

Vegetable Roast with Pasta

3 tablespoons olive oil

2 tablespoons red wine vinegar

3 teaspoons Italian seasoning

½ teaspoon salt

½ teaspoon pepper

2 zucchini, cut in bite-size pieces

½ pound (226 g) fresh mushrooms, halved

1 bunch green onions and tops, cut in 1-inch pieces

1 red bell pepper, seeded, cored, cut in bite-size

1 green bell pepper, seeded, cored, cut in bite-size pieces

⅓ cup (20 g) chopped fresh basil

2 cups (200 g) penne pasta

2 tomatoes, seeded, cut into bite-size pieces

8-ounce (226 g) package shredded four-cheese blend

This delicious medley of vegetables and pasta is fit for a king!

In small ovenproof dish, mix together oil, vinegar, Italian seasoning, salt, and pepper. Set aside.

Place zucchini, mushrooms, onion, and bell pepper in sprayed 9- x 13-inch (23 x 33 cm) baking dish and sprinkle top with fresh basil. Drizzle oil and vinegar mixture over top and bake at 350° (175° C) for 35 minutes.

Fill large pot with water and cook penne until al dente. Add tomatoes and pasta to vegetable mixture. Toss to coat, then sprinkle top with cheeses. Bake at 350° (175° C) for 10 to 15 minutes until cheeses are melted.

Polenta Bake

4 cups (960 mL) water

1 teaspoon salt

1 teaspoon pepper

1 cup (125 g) polenta

3 tablespoons oil

1 onion, minced

2 cloves garlic, minced

28-ounce (793 g) can diced tomatoes and juice

¼ cup (60 mL) tomato sauce

2 teaspoons dried oregano

2 bay leaves

1 teaspoon salt

1 teaspoon pepper

½ cup (50 g) grated asiago cheese

¾ cup (180 mL) heavy cream

Fresh parsley sprigs

Polenta is made from cornmeal and is a staple in northern Italy. It can be served as an appetizer or side dish, served hot with butter, or fried in squares.

In a medium saucepan, bring water to a boil and add salt, pepper and polenta. Reduce heat, stirring occasionally, and cook for 40 to 45 minutes or until polenta separates from side of saucepan.

In a sprayed 10- x 15-inch (25 x 38 cm) baking dish, spread polenta evenly in bottom. Cover with plastic wrap and chill in refrigerator.

In a heavy saucepan over moderate heat make sauce by heating oil, then saute onion and garlic until they are translucent. Stir in diced tomatoes, tomato sauce, oregano, bay leaves, salt, and pepper. Cook about 20 to 25 minutes until sauce thickens to consistency of thin chowder.

Remove from heat, retrieve bay leaves and throw away. Pour sauce into sprayed 10- x 15-inch (25 to 38 cm) baking dish and set aside.

Remove polenta from refrigerator and cut into long strips, 2 to 3 inches (5 to 7.5 cm) wide. Lay strips of polenta in a criss-cross pattern over sauce. Sprinkle with cheese and pour cream over top layer.

Bake at 350° (175°) for 40 to 45 minutes. Remove from oven to cool for several minutes before serving. Cut into squares and serve. Garnish with fresh parsley.

Fancy Noodles

6 cups water (1.4 L)

6 tablespoons chicken bouillon

8-ounce (226 g) package fine egg noodles, divided

1½ (337 g) cups small curd cottage cheese

1½ (360 g) cups sour cream

½ teaspoon garlic powder

⅛ teaspoon white pepper

¼ cup minced onion

2-ounce (56 g) jar chopped pimentos, drained

¼ teaspoon hot sauce

1 teaspoon white wine worcestershire

12-ounce (340 g) package shredded cheddar cheese, divided

Select plain noodles or any of the flavored noodles and pastas for a special way to serve up this tempting, tasty dish.

In a large saucepan, combine water, chicken bouillon, and noodles; bring to a boil. Cook on low heat until all liquid is absorbed into the noodles, about 25 minutes.

In a large bowl, combine cottage cheese, sour cream, garlic powder, pepper, onion, pimentos, hot sauce, and worcestershire; mix well. Stir in the noodles.

Place half the noodles mixture in a buttered 3-quart (3 L) baking dish and top with half the shredded cheese. Add remaining noodle mixture and top with remaining cheese. Let marinate at room temperature for 2 hours.

Bake covered at 325° (160° C) for 1 hour. Remove cover and bake an additional 10 minutes.

Veggie Couscous

½ cup (90 g) chopped crooked neck or
    yellow squash

½ cup (90 g) chopped zucchini

½ bunch green onions with tops, chopped

¼ cup (25 g) chopped celery

¼ cup (45 g) chopped red bell pepper

2 cloves garlic, minced

3 tablespoons olive oil

14-ounce (396 g) can garbanzos, drained

¼ teaspoon cayenne

½ teaspoon cumin

½ teaspoon curry powder

½ teaspoon salt

¼ teaspoon pepper

3 cups (750 g) cooked couscous

3 tablespoons butter, melted

Fresh parsley

For a change of pace, forget rice or potatoes and lighten up dinner with this delightful, colorful dish.

Saute over low heat squash, zucchini, onions, celery, bell pepper and garlic in oil until tender. Stir in garbanzos and seasonings and simmer to mix flavors for several minutes.

Add couscous and stir to mix. Continue to simmer while stirring to mix. Pour into sprayed baking dish and drizzle butter over top. Bake at 350° (175° C) for 15 minutes until hot. Garnish with minced green onions or fresh parsley.

Southwestern Risotto

¼ cup (60 mL) olive oil

1 bunch green onions and tops, chopped

½ cup (85 g) chopped red bell pepper

½ cup (85 g) chopped green bell pepper

½ cup (85 g) chopped yellow bell pepper

1½ cups (335 g) uncooked arborio rice

½ cup (120 mL) tequila

2 10-ounce (600 mL) cans chicken broth

16-ounce (453 g) package frozen whole kernel corn, thawed

8-ounce (226 g) package cream cheese

Here is a change of pace, and delicious too!

In a large skillet, heat oil and saute onion, celery, and bell pepper until vegetables are tender. Push vegetables to outside edges of skillet, turn up heat, and add rice to the center.

Toast the rice, toss, and stir until rice grains look translucent. Add tequila and cook until tequila has evaporated and been absorbed. Pour ½ cup chicken broth into rice and cook until liquid is absorbed. Add corn and stir in with rice.

Drop a few cubes of cream cheese in rice, stir as cheese melts and combines with rice. Continue to add remaining cream cheese and coat all rice with melted cheese.

Serve immediately or pour into a sprayed casserole dish, cool and refrigerate. To serve, reheat at 350° (175° C) for 15 to 20 minutes or until heated throughout.

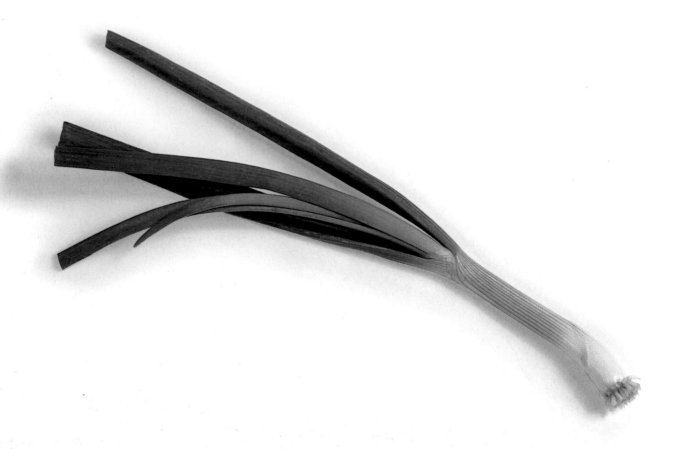

Wild Rice with Hazelnuts

1 cup (140 g) hazelnuts, husked, chopped

1 cup (225 g) wild rice, rinsed

4 cups (960 mL) chicken broth

1 cup (225 g) white rice

¼ teaspoon salt

¼ teaspoon pepper

5 green onion tops, chopped

1 tablespoon butter

The hazelnuts give a European touch to the wild rice. Not all grocery stores carry these nuts so you may have to go to a gourmet shop to find them, but the sweet, rich flavor is worth the extra effort.

Spread hazelnuts onto baking sheet and toast in oven at 250° (120° C) for 10 to 15 minutes. Remove from oven and set aside.

Add wild rice to boiling chicken broth and stir. Reduce heat to simmer, cover and cook 20 minutes. Stir in white rice, cover and simmer about 20 to 25 minutes until liquid has been absorbed. Season with salt and pepper.

Saute green onions in butter until tender, stirring occasionally. Stir in hazelnuts just to warm and pour into rice. Stir well and pour into serving bowl.

Spinach-Rice Casserole

10-ounce (283 g) package frozen spinach, cooked, drained

3 cups (750 g) cooked rice

8-ounce (226 g) package shredded cheddar cheese

2 tablespoons minced onion

5 eggs, beaten

1 cup (240 mL) milk

½ stick (60 g) butter, melted

1 tablespoon worcestershire sauce

1 teaspoon rosemary

1 teaspoon thyme

½ teaspoon marjoram

1 teaspoon salt

This casserole makes a great dish to serve with beef, pork, or chicken, and is a great "make ahead" dish.

Drain spinach thoroughly to remove all liquid. Mix together spinach, rice, cheese, and onion.

In a separate bowl, combine eggs, milk, butter, worcestershire sauce, and all seasonings. Add to spinach mixture and stir to mix.

Pour into sprayed 2-quart baking dish. Bake at 350° (175° C) for 30 minutes or until heated thoroughly.

Double-Rice Casserole

¾ cup (90 g) pine nuts

3 tablespoons orange juice

1 cup (170 g) dried currants

1 cup (225 g)brown rice

1 cup (225 g) wild rice

2 tablespoons grated orange zest

2 tablespoons snipped parsley

4 tablespoons olive oil

1 teaspoon salt

½ teaspoons pepper

⅓ cup (30 g) grated parmesan cheese

Fresh parsley

The pungent flavor of pine nuts is the perfect addition to plain rice. They are also a good a addition to vegetable and salads.

Spread out pine nuts over baking sheet and bake at 250º (120º C) for 10 to 15 minutes, stirring once. Remove from oven and set aside. Pour orange juice over currants and set aside.

Cook brown rice and wild rice according to package directions and mix together in separate bowl. To rice mixture, add pine nuts, currants, orange zest, parsley, olive oil, salt, and pepper. Mix thoroughly.

Spoon mixture in sprayed baking dish, cover with aluminum foil and bake at 350º (175º C) for 20 to 25 minutes until well heated. Sprinkle with parmesan cheese and fresh parsley.

Herb Wild Rice Stuffing

3 to 4 tablespoons butter

1 cup (100 g) chopped celery

1 cup (150 g) chopped green onions and tops

2 cloves garlic, minced

3 tablespoons dry white wine

2 tablespoons maple syrup

1 teaspoon sage

1 teaspoon salt

½ teaspoon tarragon

½ teaspoon poultry seasoning

½ teaspoon thyme

¾ cup (190 g) cooked wild rice

8 cups (720 g) plain, dry bread cubes

½ cup (85 g) dried cranberries

½ to 1 cup (120 to 240 mL) chicken stock

3 tablespoons chopped fresh parsley

½ teaspoon black pepper

Here's a new twist on an old favorite. This stuffing will soon become a family favorite, and can be served with chicken, turkey, pork, or beef.

In large skillet melt butter and saute celery, onion, and garlic until onion is translucent. Add wine, bring to a boil, reduce heat, and simmer for several minutes.

Stir in maple syrup, sage, salt, tarragon, poultry seasoning, and thyme, and mix well. Taste to see if salt is needed.

In a separate bowl, combine wild rice, bread cubes, cranberries, and toss to mix well. Add onion mixture and stir. Slowly pour in small amount of chicken stock and stir. Mixture should be moist and soupy. (It will dry as it cooks.) Stir in parsley and pepper.

Pour into a sprayed baking dish and bake at 350° (175° C) for 20 to 25 minutes or until heated throughout and golden brown on top.

Vegetable Casseroles

*C*asseroles are a wonderful way to create flavorful vegetable side dishes. Some of the recipes in this chapter feature a single vegetable (the Cheesy Asparagus recipe below or the Easy Carrot Casserole on page 60, for instance), while others, such as the Vegetable Bake on page 92 and the Corn Pudding Casserole on page 62, use a medley of vegetables. Although following a recipe can be a hassle-free way of cooking, there's no crime in substituting or adding veggies to customize your casseroles, especially when your favorites are in season.

Cheesy Asparagus

2 15-ounce (400 g) cans asparagus spears, liquid reserved

½ stick (120 g) butter

5 tablespoons flour

Salt and pepper to taste

½ cup (120 mL) milk

½ teaspoon worcestershire

Dash cayenne pepper

4 eggs, boiled, sliced

¼ pound (113 g) cheddar cheese, cubed

½ cup (40 g) almonds, sliced

1 cup (175 g) crushed Ritz cracker crumbs

Asparagus is often reserved as a special, company dish, but your family will ask for this casserole on a regular basis.

Reserve ¾ cup (180 mL) asparagus liquid and set asparagus aside. In saucepan melt the butter and gradually blend in flour until smooth, adding salt and pepper.

Slowly add asparagus liquid and milk, stirring until thickened and smooth. You may add more milk if liquid is too thick. Add worcestershire sauce and cayenne pepper.

Layer the casserole in an 8- x 11-inch (20 x 28 cm) baking pan as follows: asparagus, eggs, cheese, almonds and repeat layers. Spoon sauce over layers. Sprinkle cracker crumbs over casserole and bake at 350° (175° C) for 20 to 25 minutes.

Broccoli Casserole Amandine

2 10-ounce (283 g) packages frozen chopped broccoli

3 tablespoons butter

2 tablespoons flour

2 cups (480 mL) milk

¾ cup (60 g) grated parmesan

1 teaspoon salt

¼ teaspoon ground pepper

¼ pound (113 g) mushrooms, sliced

½ cup (40 g) chopped almonds

4 slices cooked bacon, crumbled

½ cup (90 g) buttered breadcrumbs

Dash paprika

President Bush (the father) is the only person in the world who doesn't like broccoli – and it is so healthy, but don't tell the kids.

Cook broccoli according to package directions; drain. Place broccoli in a sprayed baking dish.

In a saucepan, melt butter and blend in flour. Add milk and cook until thick, stirring constantly. Add cheese and stir until melted. Season with salt and pepper and add mushrooms.

Remove from heat and pour sauce into a sprayed 2-quart (2 L) baking dish. Put almonds and bacon on top of broccoli. Sprinkle with breadcrumbs and paprika. Bake at 350° (175° C) for 20 minutes.

Broccoli-Corn Casserole

16-ounce (453 g) package frozen chopped broccoli

10-ounce (283 g) package frozen cream-style corn

10½-ounce (297 g) can cream of mushroom soup

1 egg, beaten

1½ cups (75 g) herb-seasoned stuffing mix, divided

½ stick (60 g) butter, melted

1 onion, chopped

⅔ cup (70 g) grated cheddar cheese

Everybody loves broccoli and corn, but when you add seasoned stuffing, butter and cheese – wow – what a combination! Family will love it and guests will be asking for the recipe.

Prepare broccoli and corn as package directs. Combine broccoli, corn, soup, egg, half the stuffing mix, butter, and onion. Pour into sprayed 1½-quart (1.5 L) baking dish.

Sprinkle remaining stuffing mix over mixture, then sprinkle cheese. Bake at 350° (175° C) for 25-30 minutes or until heated.

Crowned Artichokes

6 to 8 cans artichoke bottoms, drained

1 large clove garlic

4 tablespoons minced green onion

2 tablespoons butter

10-ounce (283 g) package frozen chopped spinach, cooked, drained

3 tablespoons sour cream

3 tablespoons mayonnaise

½ teaspoon salt

4 ounces (113 g) Boubel cheese

The artichoke was once prized by ancient Romans as food of the nobility. Play queen for the day and share a real treat with your subjects!

Rub artichoke with garlic and place in sprayed baking dish. Finely mince garlic and sprinkle a small amount on artichoke bottoms. In a skillet sauté onion in butter until tender.

Roll cooked spinach in paper towels to drain thoroughly. Add spinach, sour cream, mayonnaise and salt. Pour over artichoke bottoms.

Cut cheese into 10 thin slices and then cut each slice into 3 to 4 strips. Lay strips over spinach and crisscross in a lattice design. Bake at 350° (175° C) for 20 minutes or until cheese melts. Cut into small squares and let stand 5 minutes before serving.

Broccoli-Rice Bake

10-ounce (283 g) package frozen broccoli florets

16-ounce (453 g) package frozen broccoli florets

1 onion, chopped

2 tablespoons butter

10½-ounce (297 g) can cream of chicken soup

10½-ounce (297 g) can cream of celery soup

½ cup (120 mL) milk

8-ounce (226 g) package mild Mexican velveeta cheese, cubed

3 cups instant rice, cooked

This is a wonderful dish to "make ahead." You'll have a vegetable and a side dish all rolled up in one casserole!

Cook broccoli; drain. In large skillet, sauté onion in the butter. Add soups, milk, cheese, and rice. Heat on low just until cheese has melted.

Pour into a 9- x 13-inch (22 x 33 cm) casserole dish sprayed with non-stick vegetable spray. Cover and bake at 350° (175° C) for 25 to 30 minutes.

Broccoli-Mushroom Bake

4 slices bread

Butter

2 16-ounce (396 g) packages frozen
   broccoli spears

½ to ¾ pound (226 to 340 g) mushrooms,
   sliced

4 tablespoons chopped onion

2 to 4 tablespoons butter

¾ cup (80 g) grated cheddar cheese

1½ cups (360 g) small curd cottage cheese,
   drained

2 eggs, beaten

1 teaspoon worcestershire sauce

1 teaspoon salt

½ teaspoon pepper

*Fresh mushrooms add a special touch to broc-
coli. Cooked together with cheese and eggs,
you have a real winner!*

Butter bread and cut into small cubes to make croutons. Toast in oven at 250° (120° C) for 15 minutes or
until crispy. Set aside.

Cook broccoli according to package directions, drain,
and pour into sprayed baking dish. In skillet, saute
mushrooms and onion in butter until tender and
translucent. Drain mixture in skillet into baking dish
with broccoli.

Mix together cheddar cheese, cottage cheese, eggs,
worcestershire, salt, and pepper. Pour over broccoli
and drop croutons on top. Bake at 350° (175° C) for
20 to 25 minutes.

Southern Carrot-Pecan Casserole

3 pounds (1.4 kg) carrots, peeled and sliced

4 tablespoons butter, softened

⅔ cups (140 g) sugar

⅔ cups (70 g) chopped pecans, toasted

¼ cups (60 mL) milk

2 eggs, slightly beaten

3 tablespoons flour

1¼ teaspoon vanilla extract

1½ tablespoon grated orange rind

¼ teaspoon ground nutmeg

This is not your average carrot casserole! This dish could easily be put in the gourmet category of carrots for the "discriminating" palate!

In saucepan, cover carrots with water and boil 15 to 20 minutes, just until tender. Spread pecans over baking sheet in one layer. Bake at 250° (120° C) for 10 to 15 minutes, stirring once or twice. Remove from oven to cool.

Drain carrots and mash. Blend in butter, sugar, pecans, and remaining ingredients until thoroughly mixed. Spoon into a lightly greased, 8-inch (20 cm) baking dish. Bake at 350° (175° C) for 45 minutes.

Cheese Broccoli

2 10-ounce (567 g) packages frozen
   chopped broccoli, thawed

10½-ounce (297 g) can cream of mushroom
   soup

½ cup (120 g) mayonnaise

1 cup (110 g) grated cheddar cheese

1 onion, chopped

1 cup (100 g) chopped celery

8 Ritz crackers, crushed

½ stick (60 g) butter

Eat healthy with this easy, speedy broccoli dish.

Mix together broccoli, mushroom soup, mayonnaise, cheese, onion and celery. Pour into sprayed baking dish and top with crushed crackers.

Cut butter into thin slices and place on top of crackers. Bake uncovered at 350° (175° C) for 35 minutes.

Easy Carrot Casserole

2 cups (300 g) cooked, mashed carrots

1 cup (240 mL) milk

3 eggs, beaten

½ stick butter, melted

1 cup (115 g) chopped pecans

½ cup (100 g) sugar

1 teaspoon salt

1 teaspoon baking powder

2 tablespoons flour

¼ teaspoon cinnamon

Here's the perfect recipe to showcase the natural sweetness and bright color of carrots.

Combine carrots, milk, eggs, butter, and pecans. In a separate bowl, mix sugar, salt, baking powder, flour, and cinnamon, and slowly add to carrots.

Mix thoroughly and pour into sprayed 2-quart (2 L) casserole. Bake at 350° (175° C) for 1 hour.

Unusual Cabbage Casserole

6 cups (600 g) shredded cabbage

3 tablespoons butter or margarine

3 tablespoons flour

2 cups (480 mL) milk

½ teaspoon salt

¼ teaspoon pepper

4-ounce (113 g) can sliced mushrooms, drained

1 teaspoon butter

1 cup (110 g) grated sharp cheddar cheese

The best way to a delicious cabbage casserole is to pick the right head of cabbage. The cabbage should have fresh, crisp-looking leaves that are firmly packed and should be heavy for its size. With a cream sauce and cheese, you have a "cabbage special.

Place shredded cabbage in large dutch oven. Add boiling water to cover and boil 5 minutes. Drain. Place cabbage in a large lightly greased baking dish.

In large skillet, melt butter and whisk in flour. Cook over low heat until well blended. Gradually add milk, stirring until thick and smooth. In small saucepan, sauté drained mushrooms in 1 teaspoon butter. Add to white plain sauce.

Pour white sauce over cabbage and top with grated cheese. Bake at 350° (175° C) for 30 minutes or until cheese melts and sauce is bubbly.

Corn Pudding Casserole

6 thick slices bacon

1 cup (175 g) chopped leeks

¼ cup (45 g) diced red bell pepper

¼ cup (45 g) diced green bell pepper

3 large ears fresh corn

3 egg yolks

2 cups (480 mL) whipping cream

½ teaspoon dry mustard

¼ teaspoon worcestershire

¼ teaspoon Tabasco

1 teaspoon salt

½ teaspoon ground black pepper

1 tablespoon snipped fresh parsley

Hard to resist having corn on the menu at least once a week, but fresh corn is the best!

In a skillet, fry bacon until crisp. Drain on paper towels to cool. Add leeks and bell peppers to skillet and saute over medium heat until tender. Remove from skillet with slotted spoon to drain and place in mixing bowl. Set aside.

Heat large pot with water to boiling and carefully drop ears of corn into water. Cook for 5-6 minutes until tender. Remove from pot and rinse under cold water to cool.

When corn has cooled, cut kernels from cob and add to mixing bowl with leeks, and bell peppers. Crumble cooled bacon and add to mixing bowl. Mix well and sprinkle over bottom of a 4- x 6-inch (10 x 15) sprayed baking dish.

In a separate bowl, whisk together egg yolks, whipping cream, mustard, worcestershire, Tabasco, salt, pepper, and parsley. Slowly pour into baking dish and bake at 350° (175° C) for 40 to 45 minutes. Garnish with fresh parsley.

Cheesy Cauliflower Casserole

1 head cauliflower

¼ teaspoon salt

1 cup (240 g) sour cream

1½ (165 g) cups shredded cheddar cheese, divided

½ teaspoon salt

¼ teaspoon white pepper

The creamy, cheesy cauliflower featured in this casserole is a great way to get the kids to eat cauliflower.

Remove any brown spots on cauliflower and break into smaller pieces. Place cauliflower in saucepan. Cover with water and add the salt and boil until slightly tender.

Drain thoroughly and put half the cauliflower into a sprayed 1-quart (1 L) baking dish. In a separate bowl, mix together sour cream and half of the cheese, salt, and white pepper.

Pour half the cheese mixture over the cauliflower, add remaining cauliflower, then remaining cheese mixture. Top with remaining ¾ cup cheese. Bake at 350° (175° C) for 10 to15 minutes or until heated throughout.

Corn Casserole

15-ounce (425 g) can cream-style corn

15-ounce (425 g) can whole kernel corn, drained

8-ounce (226 g) package shredded cheese

1 green bell pepper, chopped

1 onion, chopped

2 eggs, beaten

4-ounce (113 g) jar chopped pimientos, drained

¼ teaspoon salt

¼ teaspoon pepper

½ to 1 teaspoon hot sauce

1 cup (175 g) cracker crumbs

Everybody loves corn, and this quick and easy casserole is a great way to please everyone. Adjust the hot sauce to suit your family's palette.

Mix together all ingredients and spoon into sprayed baking dish. Bake at 350° (175° C) for 45 minutes to 1 hour.

Harvest Corn Casserole

Salt and pepper

6 to 8 ears corn, cleaned

8-ounce (226 g) package cream cheese or goat cheese

4 to 6 tablespoons butter

¼ cup (35 g) flour

4½ ounce (127 g) can diced green chilies, drained

2¼ cups (540 mL) milk

Dash cayenne pepper

Dash salt

4 eggs

This hearty, colorful casserole may become your new favorite side dish. Make it for your next pot luck contribution or when you feel the need for some real comfort food.

Salt and pepper ears of corn and brown in large skillet. Cut kernels and pulp from ears and add to skillet. Mix cheese and butter and add to skillet to melt. Stir in flour in melted butter and mix thoroughly.

In separate bowl, mix green chilies, milk, cayenne pepper, salt and stir in slightly beaten eggs. Pour into skillet and mix with corn. Pour entire mixture into greased or sprayed 7- x 11-inch (18 x 28 cm) baking dish.

Bake covered at 350° (175° C) for 1 hour or until center is firm and edges are brown.

Cowboy Casserole

1 tablespoon olive oil

10 corn tortillas

¼ teaspoon cumin

2 14½-ounce (411 g) cans Mexican stewed tomatoes

4.5 ounce (127 g) can green chilies, drained

¾ cup (110 g) chopped onion

1 green bell pepper, chopped

15-ounce (425 g) can black beans, drained

1 cup (60 g) loosely packed fresh cilantro, chopped

¼ teaspoon chili powder

2 cups (220 g) grated sharp cheddar cheese

This "cowboy" has been to old Mexico and has a taste for the "spiced up" tortilla.

Pour olive oil into large baking dish. Place four corn tortillas in the bottom of the dish. Cut the remaining tortillas into strips and set aside.

Layer the tomatoes, chilies, onion, bell pepper, beans, cilantro, and chili powder in the baking dish on top of the tortillas. Top with the strips of tortillas and the grated cheddar cheese. Cover casserole with foil and bake at 400° (200°) for 20 minutes.

Green Chili Casserole

1 cup (240 mL) half-and-half cream

2 eggs

⅓ cup (50 g) flour

3 4-ounce (113 g) cans whole green chilies or 1 3-ounce (85 g) can jalapeno peppers

8 ounces (226 g) grated Monterey Jack cheese

8 ounces (226 g) grated cheddar cheese

8-ounce (226 g) can tomato sauce

Here's a great casserole to go with Mexican food or to perk up a ho-hum meal!

Mix half-and-half, eggs and flour until smooth. Cut chilies or peppers down the middle, rinse out seeds, and drain chilies on paper towels.

Mix cheeses and set aside a little for topping. In sprayed 1½-quart (1.5 L) baking dish, make layers of remaining cheese, chilies, and egg mixture.

Pour tomato sauce over top and sprinkle with remaining cheese. Bake at 350° (175° C) for 1 ½ hours or until cooked in center.

Eggplant Special

2 large eggplants

2 15-ounce (425 g) cans diced tomatoes, liquid reserved

1 onion, chopped

¼ cup (60 mL) salsa

1 egg, beaten

1 cup (50 g) seasoned croutons

8-ounce (226 g) package shredded cheddar cheese

Eggplants and tomatoes just go together. And with croutons and cheese, you have a winner.

Peel eggplants, slice, and cook in boiling water until tender. Place in a sprayed 9- x 13-inch (22 x 33 cm) baking dish.

Drain tomatoes, reserving liquid. Pour tomatoes over eggplant. Whisk together egg, reserved liquid, and salsa, then pour over eggplant mixture.

Sprinkle croutons and cheese over top. Bake at 350° (175° C) for 40 to 45 minutes.

Eggplant-Tomato Festival

1 large eggplant

1 large onion, sliced

1 large green bell pepper, sliced

Vegetable oil

2 teaspoons salt

1 teaspoon white pepper

¾ teaspoon basil

4 to 5 tomatoes, sliced

¾ cup (70 g) breadcrumbs

¾ cup (80 g) grated cheddar cheese

A little known fact: the eggplant is not a vegetable; it's actually a fruit that's related to the potato and tomato. For best flavor, choose an eggplant that is smooth-skinned and heavy for its size, and avoid those with soft or brown spots.

Slice eggplant about ¼-inch (6 mm) thick. Saute in vegetable oil, drain and set aside. Saute onions and peppers in oil and drain.

In a sprayed 2-quart (2 L) baking dish, place a layer of eggplant slices and season with salt, pepper, and basil. Repeat with layers of onion, bell pepper, and remaining eggplant, seasoning after each layer.

Place tomato slices over eggplant and sprinkle breadcrumbs and cheese over tomatoes. Bake at 350° (175°) for 30 to 40 minutes or until browned on top.

Sunday Lima Bean Casserole

2 cups (480 mL) water

4 cups (300 g) fresh, shelled baby lima
    beans or fresh frozen baby lima beans

5 slices bacon

2½ tablespoons flour

3 tablespoons brown sugar

1½ teaspoons salt

¼ teaspoon pepper

1½ tablespoons dry mustard

1½ tablespoons lemon juice

¾ cup (70 g) dry breadcrumbs

3 tablespoons butter, melted

½ to ¾ cup (55 to 80 g) shredded sharp
    cheddar cheese

*Lima beans are often overlooked in the kitchen,
but with this recipe, no one will forget the limas!*

Lightly grease an 8-inch (20 cm) baking dish. In
saucepan bring water to boil and add lima beans.
Return to boil, then reduce heat and simmer until tender, approximately 20 minutes. Drain and reserve one
cup (240 mL) of liquid.

Place lima beans in baking dish. Set aside. Cook
bacon until crisp. Drain, crumble and set aside. Save
2 tablespoons of bacon drippings in skillet. Add flour
and stir over low heat until smooth. Cook one additional minute and gradually add reserved bean liquid.

Continue to cook over low heat, stirring constantly,
until thickened. Stir in brown sugar, salt, pepper, mustard and lemon juice. Pour mixture over lima beans.
Combine breadcrumbs and melted butter and sprinkle
over lima beans.

Bake at 350° (175° C) for 25 minutes. Sprinkle top of
casserole with grated cheese and bake an additional 8
to 10 minutes. Sprinkle top with crumbled bacon.

Baked Limas

5 to 6 cups (1.5 L) water

1-pound (453 g) bag dried lima beans

1 onion, chopped

1 bell pepper, chopped

3 tablespoons butter

2 teaspoons worcestershire sauce

2 teaspoons mustard

2 tablespoons packed brown sugar

2½ teaspoons seasoned salt

¼ teaspoon seasoned pepper

10 slices thick sliced bacon, chopped and cooked

Never cook a lima without a touch of sugar — it brings out the flavor and the bacon tops it off for a delicious dish.

Bring water to boil, add lima beans, and cook for 5 to 10 minutes covered. Remove from heat and let stand covered.

While preparing recipe, brown onion and bell pepper in butter until translucent and tender. Stir in worcestershire, mustard, brown sugar, seasoned salt and pepper. Simmer for 5 to 10 minutes.

If beans are slightly tender, pour into 9- x 13-inch (23 x 33 cm) baking dish. (If they are not tender, boil for a few more minutes, but don't overcook). Pour sauce from skillet over beans. Sprinkle with bacon and bake at 300° (150° C) for 10 to 15 minutes.

Green Bean Special

2 16-ounce (453 g) packages frozen green beans, divided

10-ounce (283 g) can sliced water chestnuts, drained, divided

15-ounce (425 g) can bamboo shoots, drained, divided

10½-ounce (297 g) can cream of celery soup, divided

10½-ounce (297 g) can cream of chicken soup

½ cup (40 g) grated parmesan cheese

2 cans French fried onion rings

Green beans are the most versatile of our vegetables. You can't go wrong if you just cook the green beans with a little butter, but they are fit for a king with all of these extras!

In a buttered 9- x 13-inch (23 x 33 cm) baking dish, layer half of the green beans, water chestnuts, bamboo shoots, parmesan cheese, and celery soup.

Repeat layer of everything except onion rings, using chicken soup instead of celery soup. Bake covered at 325° (165° C) for 30 minutes.

Remove cover and sprinkle onion rings over top. Bake another 5 to 10 minutes or until onions are lightly brown.

Beans, Beans, and More Casserole

1 pound (453 g) bacon

¼ cup (60 mL) cider vinegar

¾ cup (180 mL) ketchup

1 cup (240 g) packed brown sugar

3 red onions, chopped

¼ teaspoon dry mustard

¼ teaspoon salt

2 15-ounce (425 g) cans baby lima beans,
   drained

15-ounce (425 g) can red kidney beans,
   drained

16-ounce (453 g) can pork and beans

This is a twist on regular baked beans. Each bean compliments the other. Try it, you'll like it!

Fry bacon and drain, reserving enough bacon grease to cover bottom of skillet. In same skillet, add vinegar, ketchup, brown sugar, onion, dry mustard, and salt.

Simmer until onion is tender and brown sugar has dissolved. Pour mixture into a 3-quart (3 L) baking dish and add all beans. Stir to mix and top with bacon.

Cover and bake at 350° (175° C) for 1 hour. Remove cover and cook another 15 minutes.

Baked Beans Special

1½ pounds (680 g) ground chuck or ground
   round

1 tablespoon seasoning salt

1 teaspoon pepper

1 cup chopped onion

1 bell pepper, seeded, chopped

⅔ cup (160 mL) barbecue sauce

¼ cup (60 mL) molasses

1 cup (240 g) packed brown sugar

2 16-ounce (453 g) cans pork and beans

2 16-ounce (453 g) cans ranch style beans

2 16-ounce (453 g) cans baked beans

Everyone knows that baked beans are a must for outdoor cookouts, but they're also perfect for a smoked brisket and ideal for just plain family fare.

Season ground meat with seasoning salt and pepper and saute until brown and crumbly. Drain thoroughly. Add onion and bell pepper and cook until tender.

Pour in barbecue sauce, molasses, and brown sugar, and stir to mix. Add beans and stir well to mix. Spoon into sprayed 9- x 13-inch (23 x 33 cm) baking dish and bake at 350° (175° C) for 30 to 40 minutes or until bubbly and heated throughout.

Stuffed Yellow Peppers

4 large yellow bell peppers

1 cup (225 g) long grain rice

3 tablespoons dried currants

⅓ cup (80 mL) orange juice

2 tablespoons olive oil

½ cup (50 g) chopped celery

½ cup (75 g) chopped green onions with
    tops

2 cloves garlic, minced

3 tablespoons chopped sun-dried tomatoes

2 tablespoons minced fresh basil

2 tablespoons snipped parsley

1 teaspoon ground coriander

½ teaspoon salt

¼ teaspoons white pepper

Paprika

Yellow peppers bring a lovely color and unique flavor to any dish. When "stuffed," they add a change of pace for any meal.

Trim stem tops off bell peppers and carefully remove membranes and seeds without tearing or splitting outside of peppers. Wash, drain, and set aside, reserving stem tops.

Cook rice according to package directions and set aside. Put currants in orange juice and set aside. In a skillet, heat oil and saute celery, onion, and garlic until tender, stirring occasionally.

While celery-onion mixture is simmering, remove currants from orange juice and drain. Add currants, sun-dried tomatoes, basil, parsley, coriander, salt, and pepper and stir to mix. Stir in rice and mix all ingredients thoroughly. Spoon rice filling into each pepper and replace tops.

Arrange peppers next to each other in a sprayed baking dish. Cover dish and bake at 350° (175° C) for 30 to 35 minutes or until outside of peppers are tender. Remove from oven, uncover, and sprinkle lightly with paprika. Return to oven and bake an additional 10 to 15 minutes until top is lightly browned.

Sweet Onion Casserole

3 tablespoons butter

4 cups sweet Vidalia onion wedges

5-ounce (141 mL) can evaporated milk

1¼ cups (300 mL) chicken broth

⅓ cup (45 g) flour

½ teaspoon salt

¼ teaspoon pepper

1¾ cups (190 g) sharp cheddar cheese, divided

¾ cup (90 g) slivered almonds

1 cup (50 g) soft breadcrumbs

Vidalia onions are the best! Raw or cooked, they add the right touch to any meal.

In large skillet, melt butter over medium high heat. Add onion and and saute 10 minutes.

In bowl, stir together milk, chicken broth, flour, salt, and pepper. Pour over onion mixture. Cook over medium heat, stirring constantly, until mixture is thick and bubbly. Remove onions from heat and stir in 1 cup cheese.

Pour into a lightly greased 8-inch (20 cm) baking dish. Sprinkle with slivered almonds and breadcrumbs.

Bake at 375° (190° C) for 30 minutes. Sprinkle with remaining cheese and bake 5 minutes more or until cheese melts. Let casserole rest for 5 minutes before serving.

Creamy Potato Mix

1 pound (453 g) leeks

2 tablespoons butter

8-ounce (225 g) package cream cheese, cubed, softened

1½ teaspoon salt

1 teaspoon pepper

¼ teaspoon nutmeg

3 eggs, slightly beaten

1 cup (240 mL) milk

2 pounds (907 g) baking potatoes, peeled, grated

4-ounce (113 g) jar chopped pimientos, drained well

3 cups (260 g) grated gruyere cheese

This one-of-a-kind casserole is incredibly delicious. The cheese makes the difference.

Thinly slice leeks and discard tops. Melt butter in skillet and saute leeks until translucent and tender. Remove with slotted spoon and put in bowl and set aside.

In large mixing bowl, whip cream cheese, salt, pepper, and nutmeg until smooth and creamy. Add eggs and milk and blend well. Stir in leeks, potatoes, pimientos, and cheese and mix well.

Pour mixture into sprayed 9- x 13-inch (23 x 33 cm) baking dish. Bake at 350° (175° C) for 50 to 55 minutes or until potatoes are fork tender and golden brown on top.

Banquet Mushroom and Potatoes

6 potatoes

Salt

½ stick (60 g) butter, divided

8 ounces (226 g) portobello mushrooms, sliced

8 ounces (226 g) shiitake mushrooms, stemmed, sliced

½ teaspoon seasoned salt

¼ cup chopped chives

⅓ cup (30 g) grated parmesan cheese

¼ teaspoon white pepper

¼ cup (60 mL) olive oil

Portobello and shiitake mushrooms make the lowly potato stand out in this casserole.

Wash and peel potatoes, then cut in ⅛-inch (3 mm) slices. In a large saucepan, with a little salt, bring water to boil and blanch potatoes for 3 minutes. Drain and pat slices dry with paper towels.

Melt half the butter in a skillet. Saute the portobello mushrooms until tender. Remove mushrooms to a bowl. With remaining butter, saute the shiitake mushrooms. Add the portobello mushrooms and cook. Season with seasoned salt and pepper and stir in the chives.

In a buttered 3-quart (3 L) baking dish, layer one-fourth of the potatoes in an overlapping spiral. Top with one-third of the mushrooms and sprinkle 2 table-spoons of the parmesan cheese. Drizzle with 1 or 2 tablespoons of olive oil.

Repeat layer twice, ending with potato slices and drizzle remaining oil. Cover and bake at 375° (190° C) for 1 hour or until potatoes are tender. After the hour cooking time, remove cover and brown potatoes. Let stand 5 to 10 minutes before serving.

Arugula-Tipped Potatoes

3 to 4 cloves garlic

¼ cup (60 mL) olive oil, divided

Salt

White pepper

3 pounds (1.4 kg) baking potatoes

2 14-ounce (395 g) cans chicken broth

2 bunches argula, washed

4 tablespoons butter, divided

2 cups (480 mL) milk, divided

Fresh parsley

Fresh green onions with tops

Paprika

Try a different taste for a mashed potato favorite.

Place garlic cloves on aluminum foil. Coat with small amount olive oil and sprinkle with salt and pepper. Loosely close foil. Place in small baking dish and bake at 350° (175° C) for 30 to 40 minutes until garlic is soft. Remove from oven to cool. Set aside.

Wash potatoes thoroughly and peel. (It's acceptable to leave peel on the potatoes and many people prefer them with peels.) Cut into large chunks, put in large saucepan, and cover with chicken broth and water. Bring broth to boil, reduce heat slightly and cook for 25 to 30 minutes until potatoes are soft.

Wash argula thoroughly to remove all grit in leaves. Hold bottom of argula with tongs and dip the leaves into boiling broth of potatoes. Drain on power towels, pull leaves apart and pat dry. Snip larger leaves into smaller pieces and set aside.

When potatoes are soft enough to mash with a fork, drain and remove from saucepan. Empty water from pan and return pan to heat for a few seconds just to dry out all water.

Remove from heat and add potatoes. Mash with fork until all lumps are gone. Squeeze roasted garlic from outer skins and mash on separate plate. Add garlic and half the butter to potatoes and stir to mix. Continue mashing to remove all lumps.

Slowly pour milk into potatoes, stirring constantly. Use the amount of milk necessary for the consistency of mashed potatoes you want: more milk for creamy, less milk for drier.

Drizzle potatoes with olive oil and add salt and white pepper generously. Add half the argula and taste. Adjust salt, pepper, butter and add more argula to taste. Garnish with any remaining argula, parsley or green onions with tops. Sprinkle with paprika, if desired.

Potatoes Gruyere

3 pounds (1.4 kg) potatoes, peeled and quartered

1 teaspoon salt

¼ teaspoon black pepper

¼ teaspoon nutmeg

14-ounce (396 g) can chicken broth

2 cups (170 g) shredded gruyere cheese, divided

4 tablespoons butter

The mild and delicious cheese used in this recipe gives the potatoes a real boost!

Preheat oven to 450° (230° C). Slice potatoes paper thin. Sprinkle with salt, pepper and nutmeg to stir gently. Make three layers of potatoes and cheese, then pour chicken broth over all layers. Dot with butter on top.

Bake covered for 20 minutes then reduce temperature to 350° (175° C) and bake for about 1½ hours or until top is golden brown.

Potato Magic

1 onion, quartered

1 cup (110 g) grated cheddar cheese

¼ cup (60 g) butter, melted

½ cup (120 mL) milk

3 eggs

2 teaspoons salt

¼ teaspoon pepper

¼ cup (15 g) snipped fresh parsley

3 potatoes, peeled and quartered

Mashed potatoes may be made in many different versions and this taste treat is no disappointment.

Preheat oven at 350° (175° C). In a food processor, add onion, cheese, butter, and chop finely. Add milk, eggs, salt, pepper, and parsley to blend. Add potatoes, one at a time, and continue to blend thoroughly.

Pour into a sprayed 1½-quart (1.4 L) casserole. Bake covered at 350° (175° C) for 1 hour.

Layered Potatoes

1 pound (453 g) sweet potatoes, peeled

1 pound (453 g) large new potatoes, peeled

1¼ teaspoon salt, divided

1 teaspoon white pepper, divided

¼ teaspoon nutmeg, divided

1 bunch green onions, chopped, divided

½ cup (120 g) sour cream

½ cup (120 mL) whipping cream, whipped

½ cup (45 g) breadcrumbs or croutons

3 tablespoons butter

¼ cup (35 g) green onion tops, minced

This makes an attractive dish because the sweet potatoes add color and a distinct flavor difference for potatoes that are a little different.

Cover sweet potatoes with water in saucepan and cook until tender. In separate saucepan, cook new potatoes, covered in water, until tender. Allow both to cool and mash in separate bowl.

Sprinkle half the salt, pepper, nutmeg, and green onions into the sweet potatoes and the remaining half into the new potatoes. Stir to mix.

Gently fold sour cream into whipped cream and stir to mix. Spoon half the whipped cream mixture into the sweet potatoes and the remaining half into the new potatoes.

In a sprayed 2-quart (2 L) souffle dish, layer half the sweet potatoes, half the new potatoes and repeat layers. Swirl a knife once throughout the dish, then sprinkle with breadcrumbs on top.

Drizzle melted butter on top and garnish with minced green onion tops. Bake at 350° (175° C) for 30 minutes or until golden brown on top.

Velvety Scalloped Potatoes

1 cup (240 mL) milk

½ cup (120 mL) whipping cream

1⅔ cups (182 g) grated extra-sharp cheddar cheese, divided

1 cup (110 g) shredded Monterey Jack cheese, divided

¼ cup (60 mL) ketchup

2 teaspoons worcestershire sauce

¼ teaspoon black pepper

½ teaspoon salt

2½ pounds (1.13 kg) peeled Idaho potatoes, cut into ¼-inch-thick (.5 cm) slices, divided

2 cups (210 g) sliced onion, divided

2 tablespoons snipped fresh parsley

Scalloped most often refers to layers with a cream or cheese sauce between the layers. With this dish, the cook puts all the "good stuff" on the potatoes for you.

In a medium bowl combine milk, cream, ¾ cup cheddar cheese, ½ cup Monterey Jack cheese, ketchup, worcestershire, pepper, and salt. Stir well and set aside.

Lightly spray a 9- x 13-inch (23 x 33 cm) baking dish. Arrange half of potatoes and half of onion in the bottom casserole dish. Spoon half of milk mixture over the potatoes. Repeat layers; top with remaining cheeses and parsley.

Cover and bake at 350º (175º C) for 1 hour 15 minutes. Uncover; bake an additional 20 minutes or until potatoes are tender and cheese is browned.

Sweet Potato Souffle

5 cups (875 g) canned sweet potatoes, drained, chopped

1 teaspoon cinnamon

1 cup applesauce

1 teaspoon vanilla

1 egg yolk

2 egg whites

2 tablespoons (30 g) butter, melted

⅔ cup (160 g) packed brown sugar

2 tablespoons flour

If a soufflé dish is not in your cabinets, just use a deep casserole dish. The cinnamon and brown sugar gives it the magic touch, while the egg whites give it the light and fluffy texture.

Process or blend sweet potatoes, cinnamon, and applesauce until smooth. Fold in vanilla and egg yolk and mix thoroughly.

Beat egg white to stiff peaks. Gently fold in egg whites into potato mixture and slowly scoop into sprayed 1½-quart (1.5 L) souffle dish (or a 2-quart, 2 L, casserole dish).

In separate bowl, mix butter, brown sugar and flour. Sprinkle over sweet potatoes and bake at 350° (175° C) for 35 to 45 minutes or until set.

Candied Yams

2 29-ounce (822 g) cans yams, drained

3 tablespoons butter

¾ cup (180 g) packed brown sugar

½ cup (120 mL) maple syrup

1 teaspoon cinnamon

½ cup (60 g) chopped pecans

This quick and easy casserole goes well with a delicious pork tenderloin.

Preheat oven to 350° (175° C). In a sprayed 9- x 13-inch (23 x 33 cm) baking dish, line bottom of dish with yams.

In a separate pan, heat butter, brown sugar, syrup, and cinnamon until sugar is dissolved. Pour butter mixture over yams and sprinkle pecans on top. Bake at 350° (175° C) for 1 hour or until glaze has formed.

Sweet Potato Casserole

3 cups (675 g) cooked, mashed sweet potatoes

¾ cup (150 g) sugar

½ teaspoon salt

3 tablespoons butter, softened

2 eggs

½ cup (120 mL) milk

1 teaspoon vanilla

1 cup (240 g) packed brown sugar

⅓ cup (50 g) plain flour

1 cup (115 g) chopped pecans

3 tablespoons butter, melted

The sweet potato is the perfect dish in the fall. It wouldn't be Thanksgiving without this bountiful and elegant casserole.

Lightly grease an 8-inch-square (20 cm) casserole dish. Combine sweet potatoes, sugar, salt, and butter until smooth.

Lightly beat eggs and milk and stir into potato mixture. Add vanilla. Pour into baking dish. In small bowl mix brown sugar, flour and pecans until evenly distributed. Add melted butter and toss with fork to make a crumble-style mixture.

Sprinkle crumb mixture over top of sweet potatoes. Bake at 350° (175° C)° 35 minutes or until topping is browned.

Spinach Special

2 16-ounce (453 g) package frozen chopped spinach

1 onion, chopped

1 stick (115 g) butter

8-ounce (226 g) package cream cheese, cubed

1 teaspoon seasoned salt

½ teaspoon black pepper

14-ounce (396 g) can artichokes, drained, chopped

⅔ cup (60 g) grated parmesan cheese

In some parts of North America, eating something on New Years Day means one will have money in the New Year. It's a great tradition and this is the dish to go with the tradition.

In a saucepan, cook spinach according to directions; drain thoroughly. Set aside.

In a skillet saute onion in butter; cook until onion is clear but not browned. Add cream cheese, cook on low heat, stirring constantly until cream cheese is melted. Stir in spinach, seasonings and artichokes.

Pour into a greased 2-quart (2 L) baking dish. Sprinkle parmesan cheese over top of casserole. Bake at 350° (175° C) for 30 minutes.

Creamy Spinach Casserole

2 10-ounce (283 g) packages frozen chopped spinach, thawed

1 large onion, chopped

2 cloves garlic, minced

½ cup (115 g) butter

1 cup (240 mL) whipping cream

1 cup (240 mL) milk

¾ cup (60 g) grated parmesan cheese

½ cup (45 g) plain breadcrumbs

1 teaspoon marjoram

1 teaspoon salt

1 teaspoon pepper

½ cup (55 g) grated Monterey Jack cheese

Nothing is healthier than wonderful green spinach used in this recipe. The cheeses create a rich, creamy dish.

Drain all liquid from spinach. In skillet, saute onion and garlic in butter until translucent.

In a sprayed baking dish, mix all ingredients except Monterey Jack cheese.

Top casserole with Monterey Jack cheese. Bake at 350° (175° C) for 30 minutes.

Spinach Hearts

½ cup (115 g) butter

¾ cup (110 g) chopped onion

2 10-ounce (283 g) packages frozen
    chopped spinach, drained well

2 14-ounce (396 g) can artichoke hearts,
    drained, chopped

2 teaspoons hot sauce

1 tablespoon lemon juice

1 teaspoon worcestershire sauce

3 cups (750 mL) sour cream

½ teaspoon garlic powder

½ teaspoon salt

¼ teaspoon pepper

¾ cup (60 g) grated parmesan cheese

¾ cup (70 g) breadcrumbs

Artichokes give this spinach a royal treatment, while the hot sauce gives it plenty of spice. Use the hot sauce sparingly if you like a blander taste.

Saute onion in butter until onion is translucent. Add spinach and artichokes and mix well. Cook on low about 5 minutes and set aside.

In separate bowl, mix hot sauce, lemon juice, worcestershire sauce, sour cream, garlic powder, salt, and pepper.

Pour into skillet with spinach and artichoke and mix well. Pour mixture into 2-quart (2 L) baking dish and spread parmesan and breadcrumbs over top.

Bake at 350° (175° C) for about 20 minutes or until heated throughout.

Spinach Bake

3 10-ounce (283 g) packages of frozen chopped spinach, thawed, drained thoroughly

1¾ cups (190 g) grated cheddar cheese

16-ounce (453 g) carton cottage cheese, drained

3 eggs, beaten

¼ teaspoon salt

Pepper

1 stick (115 g) butter

3 tablespoon flour

1 onion, chopped

This spinach is seasoned to perfection and the cheese creates a creamy texture.

Preheat oven to 350° (175° C). (Roll spinach in paper towels to drain thoroughly). In mixing bowl mix together spinach, cheddar cheese, cottage cheese, eggs, salt, and pepper.

In a 7- x 11-inch (18 x 28 cm) baking dish, melt butter and stir in flour until smooth. Add onions and stir.

Pour over spinach mixture and stir to mix well. Spread mixture evenly over butter/flour mixture in baking dish. Bake covered for 1 hour.

Squashed Tomato Bake

1 pound (453 g) zucchini, sliced

1 pound (453 g) yellow squash, sliced

2 15-ounce (425 g) cans Italian stewed tomatoes

2 teaspoons sugar

2 tablespoons flour

1 teaspoon paprika

1 teaspoon salt

¼ teaspoon white pepper

½ teaspoon basil

¼ teaspoon garlic powder

2 cups (220 g) shredded mozzarella cheese, divided

⅓ cup (30 g) grated parmesan cheese

You can't beat this combination of squash, tomato, and mozzarella cheese.

Cook squash almost covered in water in saucepan. Bring water to a boil, reduce heat, and simmer for 5 to 10 minutes, stirring several times, until squash is fork tender. Drain and set aside.

In a saucepan, pour ½ cup of liquid from the tomatoes and mix with sugar, flour, paprika, salt, pepper, basil, and garlic powder. Heat for 5 to 10 minutes, stirring several times and remove from heat.

In a sprayed 2-quart (2 L) baking dish, layer half the squash, one-third of the tomato mixture, half the mozzarella, and one-third of the tomato mixture.

Repeat all layers with remaining squash, tomato mixture and mozzarella. Bake at 350° (175° C) for 20 to 25 minutes. Remove from oven, sprinkle parmesan over top, and return to cover for 5 minutes. Let stand for 10 minutes before serving.

Stuffed Summer Squash

4 straight neck, crooked neck, patty pan, cocozelle, or zucchini squash

4 to 5 tablespoons butter, divided

2 tablespoons chopped onion

2 tablespoons minced celery

1 teaspoon salt

½ teaspoon pepper

½ teaspoon paprika, divided

¼ teaspoon nutmeg

1 cup (90 g) breadcrumbs, divided

1 cup (110 g) grated cheddar cheese, divided

1 egg, beaten

This stuffing works well in just about any type of squash. The wonderful combination of seasonings creates a savory dining experience.

Make a short cut horizontally along the center line of the squash. Gradually hollow out interior of squash, leaving about ½ inch (12 cm) inside the shell. Reserve the pulp and set aside.

In a skillet, melt the butter and saute onion and celery until tender and translucent. Add salt, pepper, 1/4 teaspoon paprika, nutmeg, and pulp from squash. Mix with onion and celery until heated throughout. Remove from heat and add half of the breadcrumbs, half of the cheese, and egg to the skillet. Stir to mix and set aside.

Rub inside and outside of squash shells with butter or dripping from skillet. Put shells in sprayed baking dish and fill each shell with pulp-breadcrumb mixture. Put baking dish in a roasting pan containing several inches of water and place in oven. Bake at 350° (175° C) for 15 to 20 minutes.

Remove from oven and sprinkle remaining breadcrumbs or cracker crumbs, remaining butter, remaining grated cheese and remaining paprika over top. Return to oven until cheese has melted and is lightly browned.

Squash and Broccoli Bake

2 pounds (907 g) fresh broccoli florets, cut into bite-size pieces

2 pounds (907 g) yellow squash, sliced

1 large onion, chopped

¼ cup (60 g) butter

2 large eggs, lightly beaten

¾ cup (180 g) mayonnaise

3½ cups (385 g) shredded cheddar cheese

¼ teaspoon pepper

2½ cups (225 g) fine, dry breadcrumbs

Squash and broccoli may seem like a strange combination, but this casserole is both delicious and colorful.

Steam broccoli in large steamer basket over boiling water 5 to 8 minutes or until crisp-tender; remove from basket. Add squash and onion to basket, steaming until just tender.

Place squash, onion, and butter in a large bowl; mash. Stir in broccoli, eggs, mayonnaise, cheese, and pepper. Spoon into lightly sprayed 9- x 11-inch (23 x 33 cm) baking dish.

Sprinkle evenly with breadcrumbs. Bake at 350° (175° C) for 30 minutes or until lightly golden brown.

Squash-Zucchini Surprise

4 yellow squash, cubed

4 zucchini, cubed

1 onion, chopped

1 teaspoon black pepper

1 teaspoon oregano

12-ounce (340 g) carton small curd cottage cheese, drained

2 eggs

¼ cup (60 g) mayonnaise

4 roma tomatoes, sliced

12 ounces (340 g) shredded cheddar cheese

6-ounce (170 g) box chicken stuffing mix

¼ cup (20 g) grated parmesan cheese

Fancy vegetables with added flavored stuffing produce the best of the best.

In saucepan steam squash, zucchini, and onion until tender; drain. Sprinkle black pepper and oregano and oregano on top of vegetables. Place squash mixture in a 9- x 13-inch (23 x 33 cm) baking dish.

Combine cottage cheese, eggs and mayonnaise, mixing well. Pour cottage cheese mixture over squash mixture. Add a layer of sliced tomatoes on top of cottage cheese mixture.

Sprinkle cheese on top of tomatoes. Add stuffing mix on top of cheese. Top with parmesan cheese. Bake at 325° (165° C) for 45 minutes.

Summer Squash Casserole

1½ large onions, chopped

¾ cup (132 g) chopped green bell pepper

¾ cup (132 g) chopped red bell pepper

1¼ cups (290 g) butter, divided

1 clove garlic, chopped

4 cups (500 g) yellow squash or any summer squash

2 cups (220 g) grated sharp cheddar cheese, divided

3 eggs, lightly beaten

1⅔ cups (200 g) chopped pecans, divided

⅛ teaspoon hot sauce

1 cup (90 g) seasoned breadcrumbs

The supreme squash family goes back 2000 years. It doesn't need a long cooking time and can be eaten cooked or raw. This recipe is topped off with seasoned breadcrumbs and pecans which gives the squash a crispy touch!

In large skillet, melt ¼ cup butter and saute onions and bell peppers until soft. Add garlic and heat through.

In a large pot, bring to boil water with a pinch of salt. Add the squash and cook until tender, approximately 5 to 7 minutes. Drain the water and mash squash.

Add ½ cup butter, 1 cup cheese, eggs, and the sauteed onion mixture. Stir in 1 cup pecans and hot sauce. Stir until all ingredients are well blended.

In a large, sprayed baking dish, pour in squash mixture and mix the remaining cheese, pecans, and breadcrumbs.

Spread mixtureevenly over casserole. Use remaining butter to dot the top of the breadcrumb mixture. Bake at 350° (175° C) for 45 minutes to 1 hour, until lightly golden.

Zucchini with Goat Cheese

2½ pounds zucchini, grated

½ teaspoon salt

¼ teaspoon pepper

3 tablespoons olive oil, divided

2 tablespoons chopped green onions

3 cloves garlic, minced

3 tablespoons chopped fresh basil

⅓ cup (20 g) chopped fresh parsley

3 eggs, beaten

2 ounces (56 g) goat cheese, crumbled

3 tablespoons breadcrumbs

Zucchini at its finest!

Season zucchini with salt and pepper. Heat 2 tablespoons olive oil in skillet over medium heat and sauté onion and garlic until translucent. Add zucchini and cook about 10 minutes, stirring occasionally. Add basil and parsley to stir to mix. Remove from heat and set aside.

Beat eggs and goat cheese in large bowl. Add zucchini mixture and stir to mix. Pour mixture into sprayed 2-quart (2 L) baking dish. Sprinkle breadcrumbs over zucchini mixture.

Drip remaining 1 tablespoon of oil on top. Bake at 400° (200° C) for 20 to 30 minutes or until lightly browned on top.

Vegetable Roast

1 tablespoon balsamic vinegar

2 tablespoon olive oil

4 to 6 cloves garlic, minced

1 tablespoon thyme

1 tablespoon rosemary

1 tablespoon minced onion

¼ teaspoon salt

¼ teaspoon pepper

5 red potatoes, peeled, cubed

2 onions, peeled, quartered

2 red bell peppers, seeded, cut into bite-size pieces

1 yellow bell pepper, seeded, cut into bite-size pieces

1 green bell pepper, seeded, cut into bite-size pieces

2 yellow squash, cut into bite-size pieces

2 zucchini, cut into bite-size pieces

1 cup (85 g) grated parmesan cheese

A medley of fresh vegetables combined with a flavorful marinade creates this mouth-watering casserole.

Make a marinade by stirring together vinegar, olive oil, thyme, rosemary, onion, salt, and pepper. Arrange vegetables in sprayed 9- x 13-inch (23 x 33 cm) baking dish.

Pour marinade over vegetables and stir to coat pieces. Marinate for 2 to 3 hours and stir occasionally. Discard marinade and bake at 400° (200° C) for 30 to 40 minutes. Sprinkle with parmesan and serve.

Zucchini Bake

5 zucchini, peeled, chopped

½ large onion, chopped

½ cup (40 g) grated parmesan cheese

1 tablespoon snipped parsley

1 large clove garlic, minced

½ teaspoon salt

½ teaspoon white pepper

½ cup (115 g) butter, melted

4 eggs, beaten

1 cup (150 g) biscuit mix

Zucchini is a really delicious squash. This recipe turns into a creamy, rich dish that's also quick and colorful.

Combine zucchini, onion, parmesan, parsley, garlic, salt and white pepper in mixing bowl and stir well.

Add butter, beaten eggs and biscuit mix and mix well. Pour mixture into sprayed 8- x 8-inch (20 cm) baking dish. Bake at 350° (175° C) for 40 to 50 minutes.

Vegetable Bake

6 to 8 potatoes, peeled, quartered and cooked

8-ounce (226 g) carton sour cream

6 tablespoons (80 g) butter, divided

2 tablespoons milk

1 teaspoon salt, divided

¼ teaspoon black pepper

10-ounce (283 g) package frozen squash, thawed, drained

10-ounce (283 g) package frozen chopped spinach, thawed, drained

1 egg

1 tablespoon minced onion

½ cup (55 g) shredded cheddar cheese

Here's the perfect basic vegetable casserole recipe. It's great when made as directed, but even better when you add your favorite in-season vegetables

Combine potatoes, sour cream, 2 tablespoons butter, milk, ½ teaspoon salt, and ⅛ teaspoon pepper. With an electric mixer, beat until smooth.

In a separate bowl, mix squash, 2 tablespoons butter, and ½ teaspoon salt. Set aside. In another bowl, mix together spinach, egg, onion, and 2 tablespoons butter.

In a sprayed 2-quart (2 L) baking dish, spread half the potato mixture, half the squash, and half the spinach. Spread the remaining potatoes, squash, and spinach in the dish.

Bake uncovered at 350° (175° C) for 30 to 40 minutes or until thoroughly heated. Spread cheese over top and return to oven for several minutes to melt the cheese.

Veggie Casserole

1 cup (150 g) sliced carrots

1 cup (150 g) green beans

1 cup (175 g) diced potatoes

½ cup (50 g) diced celery

2 tomatoes, cut in wedges

1 yellow squash, sliced

1 zucchini, sliced

1 small onion, chopped

½ head cauliflower, broken into florets

¼ cup (45 g) green bell pepper strips

¼ cup (45 g) red bell pepper strips

½ cup (75 g) green peas

Sauce:

1 cup (240 mL) beef stock

⅓ cup (80 mL) olive oil

3 cloves garlic, minced

½ dried bay leaf, crumbled

½ teaspoon tarragon

2 teaspoons salt

1 teaspoon ground pepper

What a fabulous combination of vegetables with a sauce to die for. Don't, of course — just enjoy!

Mix vegetables in a sprayed 9- x 13-inch (23 x 33 cm) pan. In a saucepan, boil sauce ingredients. Pour over vegetables. Cover with aluminum foil and bake at 350° (175° C) for 1 hour.

Tomato-Zucchini Pastry

2 cups (350 g) zucchini, chopped

2 large tomatoes, chopped and drained

1 small onion, chopped

⅓ cup (35 g) grated mozzarella cheese

¾ cup (105 g) biscuit baking mix

3 eggs

½ teaspoon salt

¼ teaspoon white pepper

1½ cups (360 mL) milk

This casserole comes out like a vegetable pot pie with a well-seasoned pie crust.

Spray a 10-inch (25 cm), deep-dish pie plate with non-stick cooking spray. Mix zucchini, tomatoes, onion, and cheese together in pie plate.

In a mixing bowl, beat baking mix, eggs, salt, white pepper, and milk until well blended. Pour over vegetables. Bake at 400° (200° C) for 30 minutes.

Poultry Casseroles

*I*f you find yourself in the "what's-for-dinner?" rut more than you'd like, this chapter will change your dinner routine. There's enough variety here to keep the whole family happy! Start with the South American Chicken on page 100, next try the Tortilla Bake on page 102, and then move on to the Quail à l'Orange on page 119, the Fiesta Chicken Casserole on page 120, and the Chicken Creole Casserole on page 121.

Chardonnay Chicken

3 onions, sliced thinly, divided

1 bell pepper, chopped

2 cloves garlic, minced

Butter

7 to 8 boneless, skinless chicken breast halves

Salt

Pepper

Garlic powder

14-ounce (396 g) can artichoke bottoms, halved, drained

2¼ cups (200 g) grated gruyere cheese

2 cups (180 g) breadcrumbs

1 tablespoon tarragon

¼ cup (60 g) butter

1 bottle chardonnay wine

Invite the new neighbors over and you'll have friends for life.

Saute onion, bell pepper, and garlic in butter until tender and translucent. Spoon two-thirds of mixture into sprayed 9- x 13-inch (23 x 33 cm) baking dish and spread over bottom of dish.

Sprinkle both sides of chicken pieces with salt, pepper, and a little garlic powder and place over onion-bell pepper mixture. Scatter artichoke hearts over chicken, then remaining onion mixture.

In a separate bowl, mix together cheese, breadcrumbs, tarragon, and melted butter and pour over chicken. Pour wine into dish to cover chicken halfway. Cover baking dish and refrigerate over night.

To prepare, bake at 350° (175° C) for 20 minutes; remove cover and bake another 20 minutes until bubbly and golden brown on top. Don't overcook.

Mushroom-Chicken Stroganoff

8 boneless, skinless chicken breast halves

Salt

Pepper

½ cup (115 g) butter

2 onions, quartered

½ pound (226 g) mushrooms, stemmed,
    chopped

1 tablespoon flour

½ cup (120 mL) chicken broth

½ cup (120 mL) dry white wine

½ cup (120 g) sour cream

3 tablespoons dijon mustard

Cooked rice

Parsley

A new twist for stroganoff!

Season both sides chicken with salt and pepper and cut into bite-size pieces. Saute in skillet with half the butter until lightly brown on outside.

Simmer about 5 to 10 minutes more until opaque, stirring occasionally. Remove chicken from heat and set aside in baking dish with lid to keep warm.

Saute onion and mushrooms until tender and translucent. Pour into chicken mixture and cover with lid. Melt remaining butter in skillet and add flour, stirring continuously for about 3 minutes to remove lumps. Whisk in broth and wine, stirring constantly to thicken sauce.

Cook for about 5 minutes, then add sour cream and mustard. Simmer for another 5 minutes and stir occasionally to mix and heat throughout. Pour over chicken and warm in oven about 5 to 10 minutes. Serve over rice and garnish with parsley.

Chicken and Spinach Casserole

6 to 8 boneless, skinless chicken breast halves

10-ounce (283 g) package of egg noodles

¼ cup (60 g) butter

¼ cup (35 g) flour

1 cup (240 mL) milk

2 cups (480 g) sour cream

2 teaspoons lemon juice

2 teaspoons seasoned salt

½ teaspoon cayenne pepper

1 teaspoons paprika

1 teaspoon salt

2 teaspoons pepper

1 package frozen chopped spinach, cooked, drained

6-ounce (170 g) can sliced mushrooms, undrained

4-ounce (113 g) can sliced water chestnuts, drained

4-ounce (113 g) jar pimientos, drained, chopped

½ cup (50 g) chopped onion

½ cup (50 g) chopped celery

1½ cups (165 g) grated Monterey Jack cheese

Yummy delicious – that's what it is!

Cook chicken in water seasoned with salt, reserve stock, and shred chicken. Cook noodles according to packages directions, drain, and set aside.

Melt butter in a large saucepan and stir in flour. Slowly add milk and 1 cup reserved chicken stock. Cook over low heat, stirring constantly, until thickened. Add sour cream, lemon juice and seasonings; mixing well.

Add noodles, spinach, mushrooms, water chestnuts, pimientos, onion, and celery. Spoon a layer of spinach mixture into a greased 3-quart (3 L) baking dish. Add a layer of chicken. Repeat layers and top with cheese. Bake at 300° (150° C) for 30 minutes or until bubbly.

Chicken Lasagna

1 pound (453 g) boneless, skinless chicken breasts

½ cup (115 g) butter

½ cup (70 g) flour

3 cups (720 mL) milk

1¼ cups (105 g) grated parmesan cheese, divided

1¼ cups (300 mL) dry white wine

1½ teaspoons salt, divided

1 teaspoon pepper, divided

½ teaspoon garlic powder

½ teaspoon Italian seasoning

1 large onion, chopped

3 tablespoons minced fresh basil

10-ounce (283 g) package frozen chopped spinach, cooked

16-ounce (453 g) carton ricotta cheese

2 eggs

16-ounce (453 g) package lasagna noodles, cooked, drained

2 cups (220 g) grated mozzarella cheese

This is not your average lasagna! "Where's the beef?" It's not in this recipe — the chicken reigns supreme!

Cook chicken in boiling water about 10 minutes until tender. Drain, cool, and set aside. Melt butter in skillet and add in flour, stirring constantly to thicken into a paste.

Slowly stir in milk and continue to cook until thickened. Add ½ cup parmesan and stir until melted. Pour in wine and season with ½ teaspoon salt and ¼ teaspoon pepper. Set aside.

Season chicken with remaining salt, pepper, garlic powder, and Italian seasoning. Cut into bite-size pieces and place in baking dish. Add onion and basil and stir to mix well. Set aside.

Roll spinach in several paper towels thoroughly to drain water from spinach. In a separate mixing bowl, add spinach, ricotta cheese, eggs, and remaining parmesan cheese. Stir until blended and set aside.

In a sprayed 9- x 13-inch (23 x 33 cm) baking dish, pour ¾ cup of flour-milk mixture. Arrange one-third of the noodles over sauce and top with spinach-ricotta mixture.

Add another layer of noodles and another ¾ cup sauce over noodles. Spoon chicken mixture on top, then pour ¾ cup sauce over chicken.

Cover with noodles and pour remaining sauce over casserole. Sprinkle mozzarella over top. Bake at 350° (175° C) for 45 to 50 minutes or until bubbly and browned on top. Let stand for 10 minutes before serving.

South American Chicken

4 boneless, skinless chicken breasts

14-ounce (396 g) can hearts of palm, drained

Melted butter

½ teaspoon salt

¼ teaspoon white pepper

Fresh parsley

Hungarian paprika

3 egg whites

1 tablespoon lemon juice

½ teaspoon salt

¼ teaspoon pepper

1 cup (230 g) butter, melted

This is a different chicken – fiesta for dinner.

Flatten chicken breasts slightly. Wrap each one around a stalk of hearts of palm. Brush with melted butter and season with salt and pepper.

Bake, uncovered, at 400° (200° C) for 20 to 25 minutes, basting several times with drippings. Place egg whites, lemon juice, salt, and pepper in a blender.

With blender on, slowly drip hot melted butter into blender to make a good emulsion. Garnish chicken with parsley and paprika and pour sauce over chicken. Serve.

Chicken and Rice Casserole

1 cup (225 g) uncooked rice

2½ cups (310 g) cooked, cubed chicken

½ cup (75 g) chopped onion

½ cup (50 g) chopped celery

¾ cup (180 g) mayonnaise

8-ounce (226 g) can sliced water chestnuts, drained

½ cup (60 g) slivered almonds

10½-ounce (297 g) can cream of chicken soup

10½-ounce (297 g) can cream of celery soup

¼ stick (30 g) butter, melted

2 cups (250 g) corn flakes, crumbled

Except for the chicken, these ingredients all come right from your pantry (chicken from deep freezer) to make a quick meal for a sick friend, new neighbor, or when unexpected company happens in.

Cook rice according to package directions. Mix all ingredients together except butter and corn flakes and place in sprayed 9- x 13-inch (23 x 33 cm) baking dish.

Melt butter and mix with corn flakes. Sprinkle on top of casserole. Bake at 350° (175° C) for 45 minutes.

Tortilla Bake

2 tablespoons oil

1 tablespoon minced garlic

½ cup (75 g) minced green onions

5 to 6 boneless, skinless chicken breast halves, chopped

2 15-ounce (425 g) cans chicken broth

3 tablespoons cornstarch

1½ cups (165 g) grated Monterey Jack cheese, divided

½ cup (120 g) sour cream

½ cup (120 g) mayonnaise

4-ounce (113 g) can chopped green chilies, drained

½ cup (30 g) minced cilantro

¼ cup (35 g) sliced black olives

10 to 12 flour tortillas, 6 to 8 inches (15 to 20 cm)

Fiesta time!

Heat oil and stir in garlic and onion. Mix in chicken and saute until golden brown. In a saucepan, mix together broth and cornstarch. Boil for 1 minute, stirring constantly. Remove from heat.

Stir in 1 cup cheese, sour cream, mayonnaise, green chilies, cilantro, and black olives. Mix ¾ cup of sauce mixture in with chicken and stir.

In a sprayed 9- x 13-inch (23 x 33 cm) baking dish, arrange tortillas by spooning chicken mixture into center of each tortilla and rolling with seam side down.

Pour remaining sauce over top of tortilla rolls and sprinkle with remaining Monterey Jack cheese. Bake at 350° (175° C) for 20 to 30 minute or until heated throughout.

Chicken-Crab Divan

4 boneless, skinless chicken breasts

8 tablespoons (115 g) butter, divided

8 ounces (226 g) fresh crabmeat

¼ cup (60 mL) cooking sherry

Salt and pepper to taste

½ cup (50 g) mushrooms, sliced

¼ cup (40 g) chopped onion

3 tablespoons flour

1⅓ cups (320 mL) whipping cream

1 cup (240 mL) milk

½ bunch chopped parsley

Dash cayenne pepper

Chicken and crab together can't be beat! And of course, the whipping cream creates a creamy, dreamy dish.

In skillet, cook chicken in 4 tablespoons butter until tender. Add crabmeat and cook another 5 minutes. Add sherry and allow to evaporate quickly. Season with salt and pepper. Remove chicken and crab and keep warm.

Add remaining 4 tablespoons butter to pan drippings. Saute mushrooms and onions. Stir in flour. Gradually add cream and milk, stirring constantly. Stir in parsley and cayenne. Remove from heat.

Blend in parmesan. Arrange artichoke hearts on bottom of sprayed 8- x 12-inch (20 x 30 cm) baking dish.

¼ cup (20 g) grated parmesan cheese

2 15-ounce (425 g) cans artichoke hearts, drained

Paprika

Cover with half of sauce. Add chicken-crab mixture and top with remaining sauce. Sprinkle with paprika. Bake uncovered at 375° (190° C) for 20 minutes.

Delicious Chicken Casserole

8 boneless, skinless chicken breasts

3 8½-ounce (240 g) cans artichoke hearts, drained

2 8-ounce (226 g) cans sliced mushrooms, drained

1 cup (230 g) butter

½ cup (70 g) flour

3 cups (720 mL) milk

4 ounces (113 g) grated Swiss cheese

4 ounces (113 g) grated cheddar cheese

⅓ cup (80 mL) tomato sauce

½ teaspoon cayenne pepper

8 garlic cloves, minced

2 tablespoons salt

Pepper to taste

This recipe calls for company – and the company will want to take home the leftovers.

Boil chicken in water until cooked; drain and shred. Spray a 9- x 13-inch (23 x 33 cm) baking dish and layer artichoke hearts in bottom of dish. Layer chicken and mushrooms.

In a saucepan, melt butter over low heat. Add the flour, blending well. Gradually add the milk and cook, stirring until smooth and creamy. Add remaining ingredients and blend.

Pour cream sauce over the casserole and bake uncovered at 350° (175° C) for 35 minutes or until bubbly.

Chicken-Avocado Casserole

¼ cup (35 g) flour

Salt and pepper to taste

¼ teaspoon thyme

6 boneless, skinless chicken breast halves

8 tablespoons butter, divided

1 small onion, chopped

1 cup (240 mL) dry white wine

⅔ cup (160 mL) chicken broth

1 chicken bouillon cube

1½ tablespoons flour

⅔ cup (160 mL) cream

3 avocados

Lemon juice

Oil

The outstanding avocado perks up many a dish, and with chicken, this dish is tops.

In a bowl mix together flour, salt, pepper, and thyme. Roll chicken in mixture. In a skillet, melt 5 tablespoons butter and brown chicken. Place in sprayed baking dish.

Add remaining butter to skillet and brown onions. Add wine, chicken broth, and bouillon blended with flour. Bring to a boil and cook until thick. Pour mixture of chicken.

Cover and cook at 375° (190° C) for 1 hour. Remove from oven. Cool slightly and stir in cream. Sprinkle peeled, sliced avocados with lemon juice. Place on chicken and brush with small amount of oil. Return to oven for 10 minutes.

Chicken-Cheese Casserole

Small bag ranch-style chips

12-ounce (340 g) can white chunk chicken, drained

10½-ounce (297 g) can cream of chicken soup

10½-ounce (297 g) can cream of celery soup

4-ounce (113 g) can chopped green chilies

8-ounce (226 g) carton sour cream

¾ cup (80 g) shredded cheddar cheese

When in a hurry for a quick supper, this is the recipe!

Crush chips and place in a sprayed 9- x 13-inch (23 x 33 cm) baking dish. In a large mixing bowl, combine chicken, soups, chilies, and sour cream, and pour over crushed chips.

Cover and bake at 350° (175° C) for 25 minutes. Uncover and sprinkle cheese over top. Return to oven for about 5 minutes or until cheese has melted.

Easy Cheesy Chicken Casserole

2 tablespoons olive oil

1½ cups (150 g) chopped celery

⅔ cup (120 g) chopped green bell pepper

4-ounce (113 g) can mushroom pieces drained

⅓ cup (50 g) chopped onion

10½-ounce (297 g) can cream of chicken soup

⅔ cup (160 mL) milk

½ cup (120 g) sour cream

2 cups (220 g) grated sharp cheddar cheese

8-ounce (226 g) package egg noodles, cooked

2½ cups (310 g) cooked, chopped chicken

4 ounces (113 g) pimento, drained and diced

½ teaspoon salt

¼ teaspoon pepper

¼ teaspoon nutmeg

½ cup (60 g) slivered almonds, toasted

This recipe is heavy on flavor, colorful in looks, delicious on taste!

In a large skillet, heat olive oil. Add celery, peppers, and onion and saute until tender. Stir in soup, milk, sour cream, and cheese. Heat on low until cheese melts.

Combine noodles, cheese sauce, chicken, mushrooms, pimento, and seasonings. Lightly spray a 3-quart (3 L) baking dish.

Spoon mixture into the dish and top with almonds. Bake at 350° (175° C) for 40 minutes or until hot and bubbly.

Creamy Chicken and Macaroni

1½ cups (150 g) uncooked macaroni

½ stick (60 g) butter, melted

1 tablespoon flour

3-ounce (85 g) package cream cheese

4-ounce (113 g) jar pimento

1 teaspoon salt

½ teaspoon pepper

1 cup (240 mL) milk

14-ounce (396 g) can chicken broth

3 cups (375 g) cooked, cubed chicken

A meal in itself! Now the kids will want chicken with their macaroni!

Cook macaroni according to package directions; drain and set aside. In a saucepan, over low heat, combine butter, flour, cream cheese, pimento, salt, and pepper.

Add milk and broth, stirring constantly. Heat to boiling and cook for 3 minutes, stirring constantly. Add chicken and macaroni and pour into a greased, 2-quart (2 L) baking dish. Bake covered at 350° (175° C) for 30 minutes.

Oven Baked Chicken

2 cups (480 g) sour cream

¼ cup (60 mL) lemon juice

5 teaspoons worcestershire sauce

1 teaspoon celery salt

2 teaspoons paprika

4 cloves garlic, crushed

½ teaspoon pepper

8 boneless, skinless chicken breast halves

8-ounce (90 g) package seasoned breadcrumbs

2 sticks butter (230 g), melted

This is oven baked chicken at its best!

Combine sour cream, lemon juice, worcestershire, celery salt, paprika, garlic, and pepper in large bowl and mix thoroughly. Coat chicken with mixture. Cover bowl and refrigerate chicken in bowl overnight.

Remove each piece of chicken and roll in breadcrumbs. Place chicken in sprayed baking dish. Pour 1 stick melted butter over chicken.

Bake covered at 350° (175° C) for 45 minutes. Remove cover and pour remaining butter over chicken and cook 15 minutes longer.

Chicken Tetrazzini

5 quarts (5 L) water

3 pounds (2.3 kg) boneless, skinless chicken breast halves

3 bacon slices, halved

2 ribs celery, chopped

2 tablespoons Creole seasoning

1 tablespoon salt

½ teaspoon garlic powder

¼ teaspoon pepper

2 10½-ounce (297 g) cans chicken broth (optional)

1-pound (453 g) package thin spaghetti

1 pound (453 g) fresh mushrooms, stemmed

2 to 4 cloves garlic, minced

2 to 4 tablespoons butter

¾ cup (180 g) butter, melted

¾ cup (105 g) flour

½ pint (240 mL) whipping cream

1½ cups (130 g) grated parmesan cheese, divided

A different tetrazzini – thick, creamy, and full of flavor!

Pour water into large pot and add chicken, bacon, celery, Creole seasoning, and salt. Bring to a boil, cover, and simmer for about 1½ hours.

Reserve broth and cut chicken into bite-sized pieces. Bring broth to a boil and add spaghetti. Cook until slightly tender. Drain spaghetti into separate bowl to reserve broth and set aside.

Measure remaining broth and pour into stock pot. There should be 8 to 10 cups (1.9 to 2.4 L) broth. If not, add cans of chicken broth to equal this amount. Bring broth to boil, then simmer until broth is reduced to 5 cups (1.2 L).

Saute whole mushrooms and garlic in butter and set aside. In saucepan, melt ¾ cup butter and stir in flour. Gradually add broth, stirring constantly, until thickened. Add cream and cook until it's a thick and creamy sauce.

In 3½-quart (3 L) baking dish, layer half the spaghetti, half the chicken, half the mushrooms and half the cheese. Pour half the cream sauce over mixture.

Repeat layers with remaining spaghetti, chicken, mushrooms, and top with parmesan. Bake at 350° (175° C) for 30 to 45 minutes.

Southwest Chicken Ole

5 to 6 boneless, skinless chicken breast halves, cooked, chopped

Salt

Pepper

Garlic powder

2 cups (480 g) sour cream

7-ounce (198 g) can chopped green chilies, drained

16-ounce (453 g) package shredded cheddar cheese

16-ounce (453 g) package shredded Monterey Jack cheese

1 onion, minced

4 10-ounce (283 g) cans enchilada sauce, divided

10 to 12 corn tortillas, 6 to 8 inches (15 to 20 cm)

Vegetable oil

This easy enchilada recipe is definitely a keeper!

Lay out chopped chicken on wax paper to season lightly with salt, pepper, and garlic powder. In a mixing bowl, combine sour cream, green chilies, cheeses, and onion. Add chicken and stir to mix.

In a sprayed 9- x 13-inch (23 x 33 cm) baking dish, spread a portion of the enchilada sauce over the bottom. Dip tortilla in hot oil, drain and dip in enchilada sauce.

Spoon some of the chicken mixture into the tortilla. Roll up tortilla and place seam side down on top of enchilada sauce. Repeat with all tortillas.

Sprinkle enchilada sauce and cheeses over top. Bake at 350° (175° C) for 30 to 45 minutes.

Chicken Bake

5 to 6 boneless, skinless chicken breast halves

Paprika

½ cup (115 g) butter

Salt

Pepper

2 tablespoons flour

1 pound (453 g) fresh mushrooms, sliced

14-ounce (396 g) can chicken broth

¼ cup (60 mL) sherry

14-ounce (396 g) can artichoke hearts, drained, quartered

Did you know the artichoke is an "edible thistle?" Thistle or not, they are delicious when prepared with chicken.

Saute chicken in butter and season with paprika, salt, and pepper. Place chicken in one layer in sprayed baking dish. Add flour to same skillet and stir constantly to dissolve.

Stir in mushrooms to saute and mix well. Add chicken broth and sherry and simmer 5 to 10 minutes, stirring occasionally. Pour broth mixture over chicken and sprinkle with salt and pepper.

Bake at 350° (175° C) for 1 hour. Remove from oven and spread artichokes over top. Bake for 20 to 30 minutes more.

Easy Broccoli Chicken Bake

1 tablespoon (15 g) butter, melted

10½-ounce (297 g) can cream of mushroom soup

10½-ounce (297 g) can cream of celery soup

½ teaspoon curry powder

1 cup (240 g) mayonnaise

1 teaspoon lemon juice

2 cups (250 g) cooked chicken, chopped

2 cups (900 g) broccoli, steamed

1 cup (110 g) grated sharp cheddar cheese

1 cup (90 g) breadcrumbs

Broccoli, chicken, and cheese – one of the best casserole combinations!

In a large bowl combine melted butter, soups, curry, mayonnaise, and lemon juice. Stir in cooked chicken and broccoli.

Pour mixture into a sprayed 9-inch (23 cm) baking dish. Top broccoli-chicken mixture with grated cheese and breadcrumbs.

Bake at 350° (175° C) for 25 to 30 minutes, until hot and bubbly and top is golden brown.

Chicken Enchiladas Ole

4 boneless, skinless chicken breast halves

1 bunch green onions

10 peppercorns

3 ribs celery tops only

½ teaspoon salt

13-ounce (368 g) can tomatillos, drained

4-ounce (113 g) can chopped green chilies

⅓ cup (20 g) cilantro leaves, snipped

¾ cup (180 mL) whipping cream

2 eggs

¼ cup (45 g) chopped pickled jalapeno, seeded (optional)

2 cups (110 g) shredded Monterey Jack cheese, divided

½ cup (40 g) grated fresh parmesan cheese

½ teaspoon salt

½ teaspoon white pepper

Olive oil

8 corn tortillas

You will look forward to these enchiladas all day long!

In large saucepan, combine chicken, chopped onion tops, peppercorns, celery, salt, and cover with water. Bring to a boil, reduce heat and cook on low until chicken is tender. Drain and let chicken cool.

Combine tomatillos, green chilies, cilantro, whipping cream, and eggs in blender to process until smooth. Set aside.

Chop chicken and mix with chopped green onions, jalapeno, 1 cup Monterey Jack cheese, and parmesan in a bowl. Season with salt and white pepper. Heat oil in skillet and cook tortilla until soft. Remove from skillet and drain.

Lay tortilla flat and spoon one-eighth of chicken mixture into center. Form chicken into compact form and roll tortilla tightly. Place filled tortilla, seam side down, in sprayed 9- x 13-inch (23 x 33 cm) baking dish.

Repeat with remaining 7 tortillas and pour tomatillos mixture evenly over tortillas. Sprinkle remaining Monterey Jack cheese over top. Bake at 350° (175° C) for 20 to 25 minutes until bubbly.

Artichoke Chicken Casserole

2 boneless, skinless chicken breasts

1 bay leaf

1 cup (240 mL) sherry

Salt and pepper

3 tablespoons (45 g) butter

½ pound (226 g) fresh mushrooms, sliced

4 green onion with tops, chopped

Garlic salt to taste

2 8½-ounce (240 g) cans artichoke hearts, drained, quartered

¾ cup (180 g) mayonnaise

½ cup (120 g) sour cream

1 cup (85 g) grated parmesan cheese, divided

Artichokes and chicken – a great combination!

Boil chicken in water seasoned with bay leaf, half the sherry, salt, and pepper. When chicken is cooked throughout, drain, shred and put aside.

In skillet, melt butter and saute mushrooms, green onions, and garlic salt. Place chicken, artichokes, mushrooms, onion and garlic salt in a sprayed 2-quart (2 L) baking dish.

Fold in mayonnaise, sour cream, remaining sherry and ½ cup of parmesan cheese; mix well. Top with remaining parmesan. Bake uncovered at 350° (175° C) for 20 minutes.

Zesty Chicken Bake

4 boneless, skinless chicken breasts

1 onion, chopped

2 4-ounce (113 g) cans chopped green chilies, drained

Oil

2 10½-ounce (297 g) cans cream of chicken soup

2 5⅓-ounce (157 mL) cans evaporated milk

10 corn tortillas

8 ounces (226 g) grated Swiss cheese

We eat lots of chicken so we "cheese" it up in lots of different recipes.

In saucepan cook chicken in boiling water until done. Cut into small pieces and set aside.

In skillet, cook onion and chilies in oil until tender; drain. Add soup and milk and heat thoroughly.

Cut tortillas into strips and place in sprayed 3-quart (3 L) casserole. Add chicken and soup mixture. Top with cheese and bake at 325° (165° C) for 45 minutes.

Poppy Seed Chicken

3 boneless, skinless chicken breasts

1 stalk celery, sliced

1 onion, sliced

Salt and pepper to taste

10½-ounce (297 g) can cream of chicken soup

1 cup (240 g) sour cream

¼ cup (60 mL) white wine

4-ounce (113 g) can chopped mushrooms, drained

1 cup (175 g) Ritz crackers, crushed

5 tablespoons butter, melted

3 tablespoons poppy seed

Poppy seeds make for a crunchy, munchie chicken entrée – and it's easy too!

Cook chicken in water seasoned with celery, onion, salt, and pepper until tender. Cut up cooked chicken and place in sprayed dish. Mix soup, sour cream, wine, mushrooms, salt, and pepper and pour over chicken.

Toast crackers in melted butter. Sprinkle crackers over casserole and top with poppy seeds. Bake at 350º (175º C) for 30 minutes, uncovered until bubbly.

Chicken Camarillo

6 boneless, skinless chicken breast halves

3 tablespoons butter

2 avocados, peel, sliced

½ teaspoon grated ginger

½ cup (120 mL) chicken broth

½ cup (120 mL) whipping cream

1 small onion, chopped

¼ cup (60 g) butter

¼ cup (35 g) crumbled, cooked bacon

Classy and easy – that's exactly what this recipe is!

In a skillet, saute the chicken breasts in 3 tablespoons of butter for about 10 minutes. Remove from heat.

In a food processor, blend avocados, ginger, chicken broth, and cream until smooth. Saute onion in butter until golden, then add to avocado mixture.

Place cooked chicken breasts in a lightly sprayed baking dish. Pour the avocado mixture over chicken. Top with crumbled bacon. Bake at 400° (200° C) for 20 minutes.

Creamy Chicken and Ham

3 tablespoons oil

1 large yellow onion, chopped

1½ cups (150 g) chopped celery

1 tablespoon minced garlic

⅛ teaspoon ground nutmeg

2 tablespoons flour

2 cups (480 mL) whole milk

2 cups (300 g) diced, cooked ham

2 cups (250 g) diced, cooked chicken

14-ounce (396 g) jar artichoke hearts, cut up, drained

½ cup (120 g) sour cream

1 cup grated parmesan cheese

12-ounce (340 g) package penne pasta, cooked, drained

⅔ cup (60 g) seasoned breadcrumbs

This is a perfect recipe to use up leftover turkey (instead of chicken) and ham after Thanksgiving or Christmas!

In a large skillet, heat the oil; add onion, celery, garlic, and nutmeg. Cook until onion is softened. Add the flour and cook slowly for about 3 minutes.

Stir in milk and simmer, stirring constantly until thickened. Fold in ham, chicken, artichoke hearts, sour cream, cheese, and pasta. Mix thoroughly.

Spoon into a buttered 9- x 13-inch (23 x 33 cm) baking dish. Sprinkle crumbs over top of casserole. Bake at 350° (175° C) for about 30 minutes.

Chicken Linguine

4 boneless, skinless chicken breasts

½ teaspoon salt

½ teaspoon pepper

Olive oil

4 green onions and tops, chopped

¼ cup (25 g) chopped celery

1 red or yellow bell pepper, cored and chopped

½ teaspoon cayenne pepper

1 cup chopped pecans

15-ounce (425 g) can baby green peas, drained

½ cup (120 mL) chicken broth

⅔ cup (160 mL) whipping cream

8 to 10 ounces (226 to 283 g) linguine

½ cup (40 g) parmesan cheese

A hearty dish that pleases the palate and gets rave reviews!

Cut chicken in bite-size pieces and season with salt and pepper. Heat oil in large skillet and add chicken when oil is hot. Cook chicken to golden brown on both sides, lower heat, and cook until tender. Remove chicken from oil, drain, and set aside.

Saute onion, celery, and bell pepper in skillet until onions are translucent. Add cayenne pepper and stir to blend. Add pecans, peas, and broth. Stir to combine all ingredients.

Slowly pour in cream, stirring constantly, and heat until liquid begins to thickened into a sauce. Remove from heat and continue to stir so sauce won't burn.

Fill large pot with water and a little salt, and bring to a boil. Add linguine and cook linguine al dente. Drain linguine and add to cream mixture.

Add chicken, salt, and white pepper to cream mixture and gently toss to coat linguine and chicken. Place mixture in serving bowl and garnish with fresh parmesan cheese and parsley.

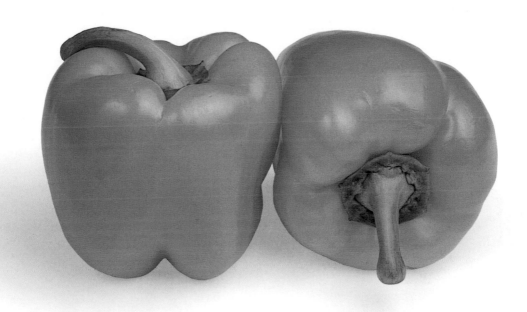

Quail à l'Orange

1 teaspoon seasoned salt

½ cup (70 g) flour

¼ teaspoon pepper

8 quail, dressed

½ cup (120 mL) oil

½ onion, chopped

½ green bell pepper, chopped

1 clove garlic, minced

1 carrot, sliced

1 cup (240 mL) chicken broth

1 cup (240 mL) white wine

1 tablespoon grated orange rind

1 teaspoon worcestershire

Sour cream at room temperature

Oranges add a zesty citrus flavor to this classic quail recipe, and their bright color looks nice in the finished dish.

Mix salt, flour, and pepper in a paper bag. Put quail in bag and shake until lightly coated. In skillet, heat oil and quickly brown quail over medium-high heat. Put quail in sprayed baking dish.

Saute onion, bell pepper, and garlic in remaining oil. Add carrot, broth, and wine. Cover and simmer for 15 minutes. Pour over quail and sprinkle with orange rind and worcestershire.

Cover and bake at 350° (175° C) for 45 minutes. Turn off heat and leave in oven an additional 30 minutes. Serve with a dab of sour cream.

Chicken in Wine

5 to 6 boneless, skinless chicken breast halves

5 to 6 slices bacon, diced

1 bunch fresh green onions, sliced

8-ounce (226 g) package whole mushrooms

6 medium new potatoes, cleaned, unpeeled, cut in halves

1 garlic clove, finely minced

½ teaspoon seasoned salt

¼ teaspoon white pepper

½ teaspoon dried thyme

½ teaspoon dried sweet basil

½ cup (120 mL) water

½ cup (120 mL) dry red wine

Fresh parsley for garnish

This dish is a French classic, but it's very easy to make. The dish can also be made ahead of time, refrigerated, and baked when ready — just add few minutes cooking time because the dish will be cold.

Place the chicken breast halves in a buttered 9- x 13-inch (23 x 33 cm) baking dish and cover with diced bacon. Sprinkle green onions over top of bacon. Place the mushrooms and potatoes around and on top of chicken, bacon, and vegetables.

In a small bowl, combine the garlic, seasoned salt, white pepper, thyme, and sweet basil. Sprinkle evenly over chicken and vegetables. Pour water and wine over entire casserole.

Bake covered at 325° (165° C) for 1½ hours. During the last 15 minutes of cooking, uncover casserole and finish baking. When ready to serve, garnish with fresh parsley.

Fiesta Chicken Casserole

4 cups (500 g) cooked chicken, shredded

1 onion, chopped

4-ounce (113 g) can chopped green chilies, drained

1 cup (240 mL) milk

10½-ounce (297 g) can cream of mushroom soup

10½-ounce (297 g) can cream of chicken soup

3 tablespoons (45 g) butter, melted

12 flour tortillas

1 pound (453 g) grated cheddar cheese

Here's a quick way to get that "Ole" flavor in a home-baked casserole.

In a bowl, combine chicken, onion, green chilies, milk, and soup. Set aside. Pour margarine in a 9- x 13-inch (23 x 33 cm) pan to coat bottom.

Layer pan with flour tortillas, chicken mixture and cheese. Repeat layers. Refrigerate overnight. Bake at 350° (175° C) for 1 hour.

Chicken Creole

1 cup (250 g) short or medium grain rice

¼ cup (60 g) butter, melted

¾ cup (60 g) chopped, blanched almonds

¼ cup (60 mL) olive oil

3 tablespoons chopped onions

1 clove garlic, minced

½ cup (100 g) sliced mushrooms

¼ cup (25 g) chopped celery

¼ cup (45 g) chopped green bell pepper

3 tablespoons flour

½ teaspoon salt

½ teaspoon pepper

¼ teaspoon paprika

¼ teaspoon cayenne

½ large tomato, crushed with juice

1 cup (240 mL) chicken broth

2 cups (250 g) diced, cooked chicken

½ cup (90 g) chopped pimiento, drained

¼ teaspoon horseradish

1 teaspoon lemon juice

Salt to taste

Cayenne pepper to taste

Fresh parsley

It will look like you worked all day on this recipe (let them think that), but actually it's very easy to prepare.

Cook rice according to package directions. Spoon into sprayed 7-inch (18 cm) round rice mold or gelatin mold. Drizzle ¼ cup melted butter over rice.

Press rice into mold so it will be tight enough to hold its shape. Sprinkle almond pieces over top of rice and pat down lightly. Set mold in pan of water and bake at 350° (175° C) for 15 to 20 minutes. Remove from oven and set aside.

In skillet with olive oil, saute onions and garlic until tender. Add mushrooms, celery, and bell pepper until tender and translucent. Stir in flour, salt, pepper, paprika, and cayenne.

Add crushed tomatoes and chicken broth and bring to a boil. Reduce heat and stir in chicken, pimiento, horseradish, lemon juice, salt and, pepper to taste. Add extra cayenne if desired.

Simmer for 10 to 15 minutes to blend flavors. Taste for seasonings. Loosen edges of rice mold, invert, and tap the bottom to dislodge rice mold in one piece onto serving platter. Spoon chicken Creole into center of rice ring and garnish with parsley.

Sherried Chicken with Pasta

6 boneless, skinless chicken breast halves

8-ounce (226 g) package bucatini or fedlini pasta

½ cup (115 g) butter

¼ cup (25 g) flour

2 cups (480 mL) half-and-half

1 pound (453 g) mushrooms, sliced

1 bunch green onions, chopped

1 green or red bell pepper, seeded, veined and chopped

¼ cup (60 mL) dry sherry

1 teaspoon salt

1 teaspoon white pepper

½ teaspoon cayenne

1¼ cup (125 g) grated parmesan cheese

This is a nice dish for dinner with friends on a special occasion. Make the dish the day before and cook it while serving appetizers and cocktails so you, too, can enjoy the evening.

In a saucepan, cover chicken with water and bring to a boil. Reduce heat and cook until chicken is tender. Drain and set aside to cool.

Cook the pasta al dente according to package directions. Drain, place evenly in a sprayed 3-quart (3 L) baking dish and set aside. When chicken has cooked, cube or chop into small pieces. Set aside to use in the sauce.

In a heavy saucepan, make a sauce by melting butter, stirring in flour and mixing well. Slowly pour in half-and-half and stir constantly until sauce begins to thicken. Stir for one minute and remove from heat.

Add chicken, mushrooms, green onions, bell peppers, and sherry. Stir to mix, add seasonings, and mix well.

Pour sauce over pasta in baking dish and bake at 350° (175° C) for 30 minutes. Remove from oven and sprinkle parmesan cheese over top. Bake for 15 minutes more or until dish is heated throughout.

Coq Au Vin

5 to 6 pounds (2.3 to 2.7 kg) boneless, skinless chicken breasts and thighs

¼ to ⅓ cup (60 to 80 g) butter

6-8 slices bacon, chopped

½ pound (226 g) mushrooms, sliced

12 to 16 small boiling onions, peeled

2 cloves garlic, minced

2 bay leaves

1 tablespoon thyme

1 tablespoon seasoned salt

1 teaspoon pepper

This classic French dish moves away from the traditional "white wine with chicken" rule to give the chicken a robust flavor enhancement. Breaking the rules for this dish is well worth it.

Remove all skin and fat from chicken pieces, rinse, and pat dry. In a heavy skillet melt butter and brown chicken on all sides.

Cook the bacon at the same time as the chicken and spoon both into a baking dish, undrained. Add to the skillet mushrooms, onions, garlic, bay leaves, salt, and pepper and saute until onions and mushrooms are translucent and tender. Spoon over chicken in baking dish.

Heat brandy in saucepan and pour brandy over the

⅓ cup (80 mL) brandy

4 to 5 cups (960 to 1200 mL) dry red wine, divided

chicken and vegetables. Quickly light with a match and allow the flame to go out. Add 4 cups red wine, cover and bake at 350° (175° C) for 1 hour or until chicken is tender and cooked throughout. After 30 minutes, check liquid in dish, and add more red wine if needed.

Italiano Chicken

6 chicken breast halves, boneless, skinless

1½ cups (360 mL) orange juice

¾ cup (180 mL) white wine

2 tablespoons Italian seasoning

½ teaspoon black pepper

2 onions, chopped

3 ribs celery, sliced

1 cup (75 g) sliced, fresh mushrooms

1 tablespoon olive oil

Paprika

Brown rice

There are so many ways to "dress up a chicken" for dinner. In this recipe, orange juice and white wine with a touch of Italian seasoning make this dish really special. Serve plenty crusty Italian bread with this dinner.

Place chicken breasts in a buttered, large shallow baking dish. In a small bowl, combine orange juice and wine; pour over chicken. Sprinkle with the Italian seasoning and pepper.

Bake uncovered at 350° (175° C) for 25 minutes. While chicken is baking, saute the onion, celery, and mushrooms in oil until onion is translucent.

After the 25-minute cooking time, spoon vegetables over chicken and bake uncovered for one hour.

Before serving, sprinkle paprika over chicken and vegetables. Serve over brown rice.

Meat Casseroles

*C*asseroles are one of the best ways to maximize the savory flavors of meat, herbs, and vegetables. The casseroles in this chapter are easy to prepare and even taste wonderful as leftovers. Best of all, many of the recipes in this chapter are one-dish meals, which means that once you put the casserole in the oven, you can relax until it's time to announce dinner. This chapter features a wide variety of recipes, including a Lamb and Eggplant Casserole (below), a Spaghetti Casserole (page 127), a Mexican Ole Casserole (page 132), and even a Ham and Asparagus Sensation Casserole (page 145).

Lamb and Eggplant Casserole

1 pound (453 g) ground lamb

1 large eggplant

1 large tomato, chopped

½ cup (75 g) chopped green onions with tops

1½ teaspoons salt

½ teaspoon curry powder

½ teaspoon paprika

4 tablespoons snipped parsley

Lamb and eggplant make for a nice change of pace from chicken and beef!

Brown ground lamb in skillet, drain on paper towel, and set aside to cool. Peel and chop finely one eggplant.

Combine lamb, eggplant, tomatoes, onions, salt, curry powder, paprika, and parsley and stir to mix thoroughly.

Spoon the mixture into a sprayed baking dish and spread evenly in dish. Bake at 350° (175° C) for 30 to 40 minutes until top is brown.

Baked Spaghetti

8 ounces (226 g) spaghetti

1 pound (453 g) ground beef

1 green bell pepper, chopped

1 onion, chopped

10½-ounce (297 g) can tomato bisque soup

15-ounce (425 g) can tomato sauce

⅔ cup (160 mL) water

½ teaspoon salt

2 teaspoons Italian seasoning

8-ounce (226 g) can whole kernel corn,
    drained

4-ounce (113 g) can black sliced olives,
    drained

8-ounce (226 g) package shredded cheddar
    cheese

Prepare this dish in the morning when you are fresh and energetic (hopefully), and supper will be ready to bake when you get home.

Cook spaghetti as package directs; drain, and set aside. In skillet cook beef, bell pepper, and onion; drain. Add remaining ingredients and spaghetti to beef mixture and stir.

Pour into a greased 9- x 13-inch (23 x 33 cm) baking dish and cover. Refrigerate two to three hours. Bake covered at 350° (175° C) for 45 minutes.

Spaghetti Pie

8-ounce (226 g) package thin spaghetti

⅓ stick (40 g) butter

½ cup (40 g) grated parmesan cheese

2 eggs, well beaten

1 cup (240 g) cottage cheese, drained

2 tablespoons oil

1½-pounds (680 g) lean ground beef

½ onion, chopped

½ bell pepper, chopped

1 large tomatoe, chopped

6-ounce (170 g) can tomato paste

1 teaspoon seasoned salt

½ teaspoon black pepper

1 teaspoons dried crushed oregano

½ teaspoon garlic powder

½ cup (55 g) shredded mozzarella cheese

This is a refreshing change of pace – try it once and you'll have repeat requests.

In a large saucepan, cook spaghetti according to directions. Drain and stir in butter, parmesan cheese and beaten eggs.

Spray a 12-inch (30 cm) pizza pan with non-stick cooking spray. Spoon spaghetti mixture into pizza pan; spread evenly over pan to form a crust.

In a large skillet, place oil, ground meat, onion, and bell pepper. Cook until vegetables are tender and meat is browned. Stir in tomatoes, tomato paste, and seasonings. Heat thoroughly.

Spoon mixture over spaghetti crust. Bake uncovered at 350° (175° C) for 25 minutes. Sprinkle mozzarella cheese over top of pie. To serve, slice like a pie.

Spaghetti Casserole

2 tablespoons butter

1 clove garlic

1 teaspoon sugar

1 teaspoon salt

¼ teaspoon pepper

1½ pounds (680 g) ground beef

2 8-ounce (226 g) cans tomato sauce

8-ounce (226 g) package spaghetti

3-ounce (85 g) package cream cheese, softened

1½ cups (360 g) sour cream

5 green onions with tops, chopped

8 ounces (226 g) grated cheddar cheese

You will have calls for this recipe on family night.

In a skillet, add butter, garlic, sugar, salt, and pepper. Cook until butter is melted, then add meat and brown. Add tomato sauce and simmer, uncovered, for 20 minutes.

Cook spaghetti according to package directions; drain. Place spaghetti in a sprayed 9- x 13-inch (23 x 33 cm) baking dish.

Mix together cream cheese, sour cream, and green onions, and pour over spaghetti. Add meat mixture and top with cheddar cheese. Bake uncovered at 350° (175° C) for 30 minutes.

Holy Stromboli

¾ pound (340 g) ground beef

Salt

Pepper

1 pound (453 g) ground pork sausage

¼ teaspoon salt

¼ teaspoon pepper

½ teaspoon rosemary

2 cloves garlic, minced

½ cup (40 g) grated parmesan cheese

15-ounce (425 g) can tomato sauce

1 loaf French bread

8-ounce (226 g) package mozzarella cheese

News flash! A loaf of bread filled with meat and cheese – what more can you ask for?

Season ground beef with salt and pepper. Brown in skillet with pork sausage until brown and crumbly. Stir in rosemary, garlic, parmesan, and tomato sauce, and simmer to reduce liquid.

Cut top off French bread in horizontal slice and hollow out bread from inside, leaving crust of ¼ to ½ inch (.5 to 1 cm) shell. Sprinkle half the mozzarella in shell, then all of the meat mixture, and then the remaining mozzarella.

Replace horizontal top on bread shell. Wrap in foil and place in a 9- x 13-inch (23 x 33 cm) baking dish. Bake at 350° (175° C) for 10 to 15 minutes or until heated thoroughly.

Company Beef and Pasta

2 pounds (907 g) lean, ground round beef

Oil

2 onions, chopped

1 green bell pepper, chopped

½ teaspoon garlic powder

14-ounce (396 g) jar spaghetti sauce

15-ounce (425 g) can Italian stewed tomatoes

4-ounce (113 g) can sliced mushrooms, drained

8-ounce (226 g) package rotini pasta

1½ pints sour cream

8 ounces (226 g) provolone cheese, sliced

8-ounce (226 g) package shredded mozzarella cheese

This recipe will serve a "bunch" and tastes much better than the usual "beef and potato" fare. Just add a tossed salad and Italian bread!

In a deep skillet or kettle, brown and cook beef, stirring often with a fork. Drain off excess fat. Add onions, bell pepper, garlic powder, spaghetti sauce, stewed tomatoes, and mushrooms. Mix well. Simmer 20 minutes.

Cook rotini according to package directions; drain. Pour half the rotini into a large, deep buttered casserole dish. Cover with half the meat-tomato mixture and half the sour cream. Top with slices of provolone cheese. Repeat process once more ending with the mozzarella cheese.

Cover and bake at 350° (175°) for 35 minutes. Remove cover and continue baking another 10 to 15 minutes or until mozzarella cheese melts.

Burritos Supreme

1 pound (453 g) ground beef

1 onion, diced

1 to 2 tablespoons oil

4-ounce (113 g) can chopped green chilies, drained

1 tablespoon salt

1 teaspoon pepper

½ teaspoon garlic powder

½ teaspoon cayenne pepper (optional)

15-ounce (425 g) can refried beans

12 flour tortillas

1 cup (100 g) grated cheddar cheese

Salsa

This is an easy dish that can be made in advance, then popped in the oven when you're ready to eat. Serve it with chips, salsa, a green salad, or guacamole on lettuce.

Brown ground beef in large skillet and pour off excess fat. Add onion to meat and saute until translucent and tender. Add 1 to 2 tablespoons of oil and stir in green chilies and seasonings.

Cook 3-4 minutes to blend ingredients. Stir in refried beans and cook several minutes until well blended.

Scoop 3 to 4 tablespoons of meat mixture into each tortilla and sprinkle cheese over top. Roll up tortilla and fold ends toward the center just before the last roll.

Place in a prepared 9- x 13-inch (23 x 33 cm) baking dish, seam side down. Cover and bake at 350° (175° C) for 20 to 25 minutes or until heated throughout.

Beef Bourguignonne

3 to 4 pounds (1.4 to 1.8 kg) beef chuck or round steak, cut into ¾-inch (18 mm) cubes

Oil

3 tablespoons flour

¾ teaspoon seasoned salt

½ teaspoon pepper

½ teaspoon thyme

¼ teaspoon garlic powder

14-ounce (420 mL) can beef broth

1 cup (240 mL) burgundy wine

1½ cups (110 g) sliced fresh mushrooms

2 15-ounce (425 g) cans small white onions, drained

Cooked white rice

This hearty beef dish cooked in its own juices with burgundy wine, mushrooms, and baby onions will make everyone glad they know you.

In a large skillet, brown meat in 2 tablespoons oil. Add flour, salt, pepper, thyme, and garlic powder. Place in a 3-quart (3 L) baking dish. Add beef broth and wine; stir well.

Cover and bake for 2 hours. Add mushrooms and onions and bake another 1 hour 30 minutes. If meat becomes too dry, add equal portions of wine and water. Serve over white rice.

Mexican Ole

1½ pounds (680 g) ground round

1 teaspoon seasoning salt

1 large onion, chopped

1 red bell pepper, chopped

1 yellow bell pepper, chopped

3 cups (525 g) chopped zucchini

½ to ¾ cup (120 to 180 mL) water

1 envelope taco seasoning

1 cup (225 g) uncooked rice

1 teaspoon salt

12-ounce (340 g) jar chunky salsa

1½ cups (165 g) grated cheddar cheese

¾ to 1 cup (130 to 175 g) crumbled tortilla chips

This is supper: well seasoned, well done, and soon gone.

Brown ground round with seasoning salt, then add onion, bell peppers, zucchini, water, and taco seasoning. Stir and saute until vegetables are tender.

In separate saucepan, cook rice according to directions. In a sprayed 9- x 13-inch (23 x 33 cm) baking dish, spoon rice over bottom of dish, then add layer of beef mixture, salsa, and cheese.

Bake at 350° (175° C) for 20 to 25 minutes. Remove from oven and sprinkle tortilla chips over top. Bake for another 10 minutes.

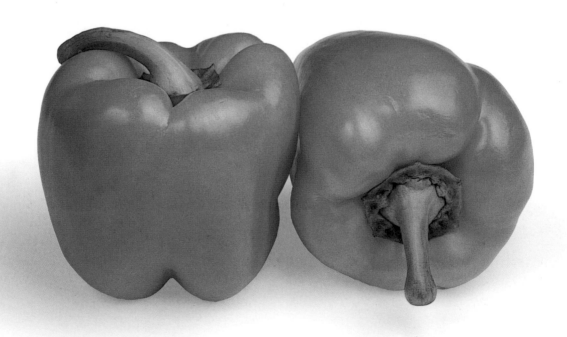

Fettuccine Italian

6 ounces (170 g) uncooked fettuccine

¾ pound (340 g) ground round or beef chuck

1 clove garlic, minced

1 onion, minced

8-ounce (226 g) tomato sauce

15-ounce (428 g) can stewed Italian tomatoes, undrained

½ teaspoon Italian seasoning

2 eggs, divided

2 tablespoons butter

8-ounce (226 g) package shredded mozzarella cheese

8-ounce (226 g) carton small curd cottage cheese, drained

1 cup (175 g) chopped fresh broccoli

⅓ cup (30 g) grated fresh parmesan cheese

Adding broccoli to this classic Italian recipe dresses it up and adds wonderful flavor.

Cook fettuccine as directed, drain, and set aside. In a large skillet, brown beef and stir to crumble. Add garlic and onion, stir to mix, and reduce heat. Drain excess grease.

Add tomato sauce, stewed tomatoes with liquid and Italian seasoning. Stir and bring to a boil. Reduce heat, cover, and simmer for 10 to 12 minutes, stirring occasionally.

Beat 1 egg and melted butter in mixing bowl. Stir in fettuccine and mozzarella cheese. Spoon mixture into ungreased 9-inch (23 cm) pie plate and press down on bottom and sides of plate to compact fettuccine mixture.

Mix remaining egg and cottage cheese in separate bowl. Pour over fettuccine in pie plate and smooth over surface. Sprinkle with broccoli. Spoon beef mixture evenly over top.

Sprinkle parmesan evenly over top and remove any cheese from edges of pie plate. Bake at 350° (175° C) for 30 minutes or until hot throughout. Let stand 5 to 10 minutes to set before cutting.

Oven Steak

2 pounds (907 g) 1½-inch-thick (4 cm) round steak

1 teaspoon garlic salt

1 teaspoon seasoned salt

½ teaspoon black pepper

½ cup (70 g) flour

¼ cup (60 mL) oil

28-ounce (793 g) can tomatoes, undrained

1 green bell pepper, seeded, cored sliced in rings

1 small yellow onion, sliced in rings

Most of the guys want beef so "here's the beef."

Remove excess fat from round steak and cut into 6 to 8 individual steaks. In a bowl, combine garlic salt, pepper, and flour. Coat steaks with flour mixture.

In skillet, heat oil until hot. Brown steak on both sides, remove from pan, and place in a sprayed baking dish.

In a blender, process tomatoes until pureed. Pour tomatoes over steak and top with peppers and onions. Bake covered at 325° (165° C) for 2 to 3 hours.

Moussaka

½ cup (120 mL) olive oil, divided

3 cloves garlic, minced

1 onion, chopped

1½ pounds (680 g) ground round or chuck

2 teaspoons basil

1 teaspoon oregano

½ teaspoon cinnamon

½ teaspoon seasoned salt

½ teaspoon pepper

2 8-ounce (226 g) cans tomato sauce

2 pounds (900 g) eggplant

Salt

2 baking potatoes

3 eggs

2 tablespoons flour

2 cups (480 g) plain yogurt or sour cream

½ to ¾ cup (40 to 60 g) grated parmigiano-reggiano cheese

This is an old-time recipe and takes a little more preparation, but its well worth it.

To make meat sauce, heat 2 tablespoons oil in large skillet and sauté garlic and onion until onion is translucent. Add ground meat, brown, and reduce heat to cook until meat is no longer pink. Drain and return to skillet.

Add basil, oregano, cinnamon, seasoned salt, pepper, and tomato sauce. Increase heat to boiling, then reduced heat to low and simmer for 15 minutes, stirring occasionally. Set aside.

To make eggplant mixture, cut eggplant into thick slices, salt both sides, and place in colander. Set aside for 15 to 20 minutes. Peel potatoes and slice thinly. In a saucepan, cover with water, bring to a boil, and reduce heat to simmer until potatoes are fork tender. Drain and set aside.

After beads of liquid form on the eggplant, use a paper towel to pat dry. Brush with olive oil and place under broiler for 3 to 4 minutes per side or until both sides are golden brown.

To make topping, beat eggs and gradually add flour while beating. Add yogurt and mix thoroughly. Make sure mixture is smooth without any lumps.

Place some of the eggplant and potato slices in one layer on bottom of a sprayed 9- x 13-inch (23 x 33 cm) baking dish. Spoon half the meat mixture evenly over the eggplant and potato slices.

Repeat layers using all the eggplant and potato slices. Spoon yogurt sauce over top and spread to smooth. Sprinkle with cheese and bake at 375° (190° C) for 40 to 45 minutes or until bubbly and golden brown.

Sunday Night Cheesy-Beefy Casserole

1 pound (453 g) ground beef

1 large onion, chopped

1 cup (175 g) chopped green bell pepper

⅓ cup (80 mL) water

1½ teaspoons sugar

1 tablespoon chili powder

2 teaspoons ground cumin

½ teaspoon dried oregano

14½-ounce (411 g) can diced tomatoes, undrained

4½-ounce (127 g) can chopped green chiles, drained

3 cups (750 g) cooked long-grain rice

1 cup (240 g) sour cream

¼ cup (60 mL) milk

1 cup (110 g) grated sharp cheddar cheese

Make this well-seasoned beef casserole on Saturday morning and it will be ready for Sunday night after a busy day off.

Cook ground beef, onion, and bell pepper in a large, nonstick skillet over medium-high heat until meat is browned; stir to crumble.

Add water, sugar, seasonings, tomatoes and chilies. Bring to a boil. Cover, reduce heat, and simmer 15 minutes. Uncover and simmer an additional 2 minutes to reduce liquid. Remove from heat; set aside.

In a medium bowl, combine the rice, sour cream, and milk. Lightly spray a 9-inch (23 cm) baking dish and spoon rice mixture into the dish.

Top with beef mixture; sprinkle with cheese. Bake at 375º (190º C)º for 10 minutes or until thoroughly heated. Let stand 5 minutes before serving.

Beefy Noodle Casserole

3 tablespoons (45 g) butter, divided

1½ pounds (680 g) ground round

⅓ cup (50 g) sliced scallions

2 8-ounce (226 g) cans tomato sauce

Dash of worcestershire sauce

8 ounce (226 g) package cream cheese, softened

½ cup (120 g) sour cream

1 cup (240 g) cottage cheese

8 ounces (226 g) noodles, cooked, drained

Here's family fare in a "stick-to-the-ribs" casserole. Your teenagers could put this recipe together.

In a skillet, melt 1 tablespoon of butter. Brown beef until crumbly. Add scallions, tomato sauce, worcestershire, and mix.

In a bowl combine cream cheese, sour cream, and cottage cheese. Place half the noodles in a sprayed 2-quart (2 L) baking dish.

Add the cheese mixture and put remaining noodles on top of cheeses. Top with beef mixture. Bake at 350° (175° C) for 20 minutes.

Manicotti Premier

2 pounds (907 g) ground round or chuck

3 cloves garlic, minced

1 bell pepper, chopped

1 onion, chopped

6-ounce (170 g) can tomato paste

2 16-ounce (453 g) cans tomato sauce

1½ teaspoons sugar

2 tablespoons snipped sweet basil

Salt

Pepper

1 cup (240 mL) water

2 cups (220 g) grated mozzarella cheese

16-ounce (453 g) carton ricotta cheese

8-ounce (226 g) package manicotti shells, cooked, drained

1½ cups (120 g) grated parmesan cheese

Always a delightful dish; just let the manicotti shells cool before trying to "stuff" – we don't want burned fingers.

Brown ground meat, garlic, bell pepper, onion, and drain thoroughly. To make sauce, stir in tomato paste, tomato sauce, sugar, basil, salt, pepper, and water. Simmer for 30 to 45 minutes, stirring occasionally.

Pour ½ cup sauce in a sprayed, 9- x 13-inch (23 x 33 cm) baking dish to cover bottom. In separate bowl, combine mozzarella and ricotta.

Stuff manicotti shells with cheeses and lay on top of sauce. Pour remaining sauce over shells and sprinkle with parmesan. Bake at 350° (175° C) for about 30 minutes.

Beef Stew Casserole

2 pounds (907 g) stew meat, cut in bite-size pieces

1 cup (150 g) sliced carrots

1 onion, chopped

4 potatoes, peeled, cubed

1 cup (100 g) chopped celery

2 teaspoons salt

1 teaspoon pepper

10½-ounce (297 g) can cream of mushroom soup

½ cup (120 mL) water

1 dried bay leaf, crumbled

½ cup (120 mL) burgundy wine

Put this recipe together in the morning, then run home at lunch (make any excuse you can), place in oven, and supper is ready at 6. It just takes a little planning!

Mix all ingredients in a sprayed baking dish. Bake at 275° (135° C) for 5 hours.

Easy Winter Warmer

Oil

Salt

6 cups (450 g) egg noodles, uncooked, divided

3 tablespoons (45 g) butter, melted

1½ pounds (679 g) ground chuck or ground round, divided

2½ cups (600 mL) spaghetti sauce, divided

12-ounce (340 g) package shredded mozzarella cheese, divided

Spaghetti sauce on noodles! Lets be creative, you don't have to have a cream sauce on noodles.

Add a drop or two of oil to water with a dash of salt and cook noodles as package directs. Drain thoroughly and coat with butter.

Brown ground chuck and drain thoroughly. Pour half of the spaghetti sauce in the bottom of a 9- x 13-inch (23 x 33 cm) baking dish. Add half the noodles, half the meat, and half the cheese. Repeat for second layer.

Bake covered at 300° (150° C) until cheese melts and dish is heated throughout.

Beef Pappardelle

8-ounce (226 g) package pappardelle, radiatore, ricciolini or rigatoni noodles

1 pound (453 g) ground chuck or round beef

2 cloves garlic, minced

½ teaspoon pepper

1 teaspoon seasoning salt

6-ounce (170 g) can tomato paste

3 cups (720 mL) water

1½-ounce (42 g) envelope spaghetti sauce mix

½ teaspoon crushed dried thyme

3-ounce (85 g) package cream cheese, softened

8-ounce (226 g) carton sour cream

¾ cup (60 g) grated parmesan cheese, divided

2 tablespoons snipped parsley

Ground beef at its best!

In large saucepan filled with water, cook noodles according to package directions. Drain and set aside.

In skillet brown ground chuck until crumbly and cooked throughout. Stir in garlic and saute until tender and translucent. Drain beef in skillet, season with pepper and seasoning salt, and stir to mix. Set aside.

In mixing bowl combine tomato paste, water, spaghetti sauce mix, and thyme. Stir to mix thoroughly. Pour tomato sauce into beef mixture, bring to a boil, and reduce heat to simmer for 20 to 25 minutes.

In a 3-quart (3 L) sprayed baking dish, spread half the cooked noodles over the bottom. Spoon half the tomato sauce-beef mixture over noodles.

In a separate bowl, combine cream cheese, sour cream, ⅓ cup parmesan, and parsley. Stir to mix. Spoon half the cream cheese over tomato sauce-beef mixture.

Layer remaining noodles on top, then remaining tomato sauce-beef mixture and final layer of cream cheese.

Sprinkle with remaining parmesan cheese and bake at 350° (175° C) for 15 to 20 minutes or heated throughout.

Veal Steak Ole

1 to 1½ pounds (453 to 680 g) thin veal steak

¼ to ½ cup (35 to 70 g) flour

3 to 4 tablespoons olive oil, divided

1/3 cup (240 mL) chili sauce

2 medium onions, sliced

10½-ounce (297 g) can beef broth

1 teaspoon salt

2 cups (150 g) noodles

10½-ounce (297 g) can condensed cream of chicken soup

½ cup (45 g) seasoned breadcrumbs

2 tablespoons melted butter

¼ to ½ cup (20 to 40 g) grated parmesan cheese

Parsley to garnish

Green onions with tops to garnish

This recipe makes a creamy sauce (you could call it gravy) that tastes wonderful spooned over a hot biscuit or roll.

Place veal in flour and pat to coat both sides. Cut in bite-size pieces and drop in flour and coat again. Brown both sides of veal in skillet with 2 to 3 tablespoons olive oil.

Reduce heat to low and add chili sauce, onions and beef broth. Cover and simmer about 30 minutes, stirring occasionally.

Fill large saucepan with about 5 to 6 cups water and bring to boil. Add salt and 1 tablespoon olive oil to water and slowly add pasta. Cook pasta to al dente by tasting pasta as it cooks.

When there is no taste of raw flour and the pasta still maintains some resistance to the bite, remove saucepan from heat and with a pasta scoop, let pasta drip-dry for a few seconds over the saucepan before dropping into buttered or sprayed mixing bowl.

Toss pasta with cream of chicken soup. Toss well to thoroughly coat pasta. Pour into serving bowl and spoon veal mixture around the edges of the bowl.

In the center, on top of the pasta, sprinkle seasoned breadcrumbs and drizzle with melted butter. Top with grated parmesan cheese. Garnish with parsley and green onions to serve.

Spicy Lasagna

1 pound (453 g) hot Italian sausage

8-ounce (226 g) package hot pork sausage

1 onion, chopped

3 cloves garlic, minced

2 tablespoons oil

28-ounce (793 g) can crushed tomatoes

6-ounce (170 g) can tomato paste

1½ teaspoon basil

1½ teaspoons oregano

½ teaspoon salt

1 cup (85 g) grated parmesan cheese

2 cups (480 g) small-curd cottage cheese, drained

1 egg, beaten

1 cup fresh parsley, snipped, divided

6 lasagna noodles, cooked

12-ounce package shredded mozzarella cheese, divided

Hot sausages means "this recipe has the authority" to please.

Brown both sausages in large skillet until crumbly and no longer pink. Drain through strainer and remove grease from skillet. Saute onion and garlic with oil in skillet. Cook until translucent and stir to keep from burning.

Add crushed tomatoes, tomato paste, and seasonings and stir to mix. Allow to cook until liquid has thickened enough to be spooned out of skillet and spread easily over noodles. Add sausage to the tomato mixture and stir to mix.

In a separate bowl, add parmesan, cottage cheese, egg, and half the parsley. Stir to mix. In a sprayed 9- x 13-inch (23 x 33 cm) baking dish, spoon out a thin layer of sausage-tomato mixture over the bottom of the dish.

Layer half the noodles, half the parmesan mixture, half the mozzarella, and half the sausage-tomato mixture. Repeat the layers using the remaining noodles, parmesan mixture, mozzarella, and sausage-tomato mixture.

Sprinkle the top with remaining parsley. Cover with foil and bake at 350° (175° C) for 30 to 35 minutes until bubbly.

Cheesy Stuffed Bell Peppers

6 green bell peppers

1¼ pounds (567 g) lean ground beef

½ cup (75 g) chopped onion

¾ cup (187 g) cooked rice

1 egg

2 15-ounce (425 g) cans Italian stewed tomatoes, divided

½ teaspoon seasoned salt

½ teaspoon black pepper

½ teaspoon garlic powder

1 tablespoon worcestershire sauce

2 cups (200 g) shredded cheddar cheese, divided

Stuffed peppers have to be a "down-home" special supper! In just about every casserole we make, we use bell peppers, but with this recipe you get the whole pepper with just the right "stuff" to make it delicious.

Cut off a small portion of the tops of the bell peppers; remove seeds and membranes. Place in a roaster with salted water and bring to a boil. Cook 10 minutes (they will not be completely done). Drain and set aside to cool.

In a skillet, brown the ground beef and onion; drain. Add rice, egg, 1 can tomatoes, worcestershire, and seasonings. Simmer 5 minutes. Remove from heat and add 1 cup cheese, mixing well.

Stuff the peppers with the mixture and set upright in a buttered, round baking dish. (You may have to trim little slivers off the bottoms of the peppers so they will sit upright.) Pour the remaining can of tomatoes on and around the peppers.

Bake uncovered at 350° (175° C) for 25 minutes. Remove from oven and sprinkle remaining cheese on top and return to oven for 10 minutes.

Ham and Asparagus Sensation

4 eggs

4-ounce (113 g) package almond slivers or almond slices

2 tablespoons (30 g) butter

½ cup (45 g) seasoned breadcrumbs

1 pound (453 g) fresh asparagus, trimmed

2 cups (300 g) cooked, cubed ham

½ cup (55 g) grated cheddar cheese

3 tablespoons tapioca

3 tablespoons chopped green onions with tops

¼ cup (25 g) chopped mushrooms

3 tablespoons minced red bell pepper

2 tablespoons fresh, snipped parsley

1 tablespoon lemon juice

½ cup (120 mL) milk

10½-ounce (297 g) cream of mushroom soup

Paprika

This beautiful dish is a great way to use up small chunks of leftover ham.

In a saucepan, cover eggs with water. Cook until hard-boiled, about 12 to 15 minutes. Remove from heat, drain and set aside to cool.

Pour almond slivers onto baking sheet and toast at 250° (120° C) for 10 to 15 minutes. Remove and set aside to cool.

In saucepan, melt butter and remove from heat. Add breadcrumbs and toss to coat. Set aside. Arrange fresh asparagus in steamer basket and cook in saucepan of water for about 2 to 3 minutes until slightly tender. Drain, arrange asparagus in sprayed 1½-quart (1.5 L) baking dish and set aside.

In mixing bowl stir together ham, cheddar cheese, tapioca, onion, mushrooms, almonds, bell pepper, parsley, and lemon juice until well mixed.

Remove shells from eggs and carefully make thin slices diagonally across eggs. If eggs are still warm and hard to cut, put in refrigerator to chill. Spoon a layer of half the ham mixture over asparagus and top with a layer of half the egg slices. Repeat layers with remaining ham mixture and egg slices.

In mixing bowl pour milk into mushroom soup and whisk until well blended. Slowly pour over ham mixture in baking dish. Top with breadcrumbs and small sprinkles of paprika. Bake at 350° (175° C) for 25 to 30 minutes.

Sweet and Sour Cabbage Rolls

¼ cup (60 mL) olive oil

½ cup (75 g) minced onion

½ cup (50 g) minced celery

4 cloves garlic, minced

2 28-ounce (793 g) cans crushed tomatoes

1 tablespoon tomato paste

¼ cup (60 mL) dry red wine

¼ cup (15 g) minced fresh parsley

2 tablespoons minced fresh basil

1 tablespoon oregano

½ teaspoon nutmeg

½ to 1 teaspoon salt

½ teaspoon black pepper

¼ teaspoon cayenne

1 head green cabbage

15-ounce (425 g) can stewed tomatoes

1 cup (240 mL) water

1 tablespoon lemon juice

¼ cup (25 g) packed brown sugar

1 teaspoon ground ginger

¾ cup (180 g) cooked white rice

8 ounces (226 g) ground pork sausage

1 pound (453 g) ground chuck roast

½ cup (75 g) chopped green onion with
    tops

½ teaspoon thyme

1 teaspoon caraway seeds

1 teaspoon salt

1 teaspoon pepper

1½ cups (225 g) sauerkraut, rinsed, drained,
    divided

Fresh parsley

This handcrafted casserole dish is fun to make and tastes wonderful. Best of all, it tastes even better on the second day!

In heavy saucepan, heat oil and sauté onion, celery, and garlic. Cook until ingredients are tender and translucent. Over medium heat, pour in tomatoes, tomato paste, red wine, parsley, basil, oregano, nutmeg, salt, pepper, and cayenne. Cook for 10 to 15 minutes, stirring occasionally.

Tear off 8 to 10 large whole cabbage leaves and wash. Fill large pot at least half full of water and bring to a boil. Submerge cabbage leaves in boiling water, one at a time, and cook for 5 minutes or until tender. Take leaves out of pot and dunk in bowl of cold water to cool, then drain and set aside.

To heavy saucepan containing tomato sauce mixture, add stewed tomatoes, water, lemon juice, brown sugar, and ginger. Stir to mix and set aside.

In separate bowl, mix together rice, pork, beef, green onions, thyme, caraway seeds, salt, and pepper. Stir to mix well. In a sprayed baking dish, spread 1 cup sauerkraut over bottom of dish and set aside.

On large cutting board surface or counter, spread out several whole cabbage leaves. Spoon about ⅓ to ½ cup meat filling into center of cabbage leaf. Fold one side over filling, then fold in both ends. Roll tightly to hold ends in place. Place seam side down in baking dish with sauerkraut.

Repeat process with each cabbage leaf until meat mixture is gone. Arrange cabbage rolls in one layer on top of sauerkraut, then add remaining sauerkraut.

Bring tomato sauce mixture to a boil and pour over sauerkraut and cabbage rolls. Cover with aluminum foil and bake at 350° (175° C) for 1 hour and 45 minutes. Garnish with fresh parsley and serve.

Company Beef Casserole

2 pounds (907 g) lean, ground round steak

1 teaspoon seasoned salt

1 tablespoon sugar

½ teaspoon black pepper

2 15-ounce (425 g) cans stewed tomatoes

2 8-ounce (226 g) cans tomato sauce

3 cloves garlic, finely minced

8-ounce (226 g) package angel hair pasta

8-ounce (226 g) package cream cheese

1 pint (480 g) sour cream

2 bunches fresh green onion and tops chopped

8-ounce (226 g) package shredded cheddar cheese

This is an everyday family meal made special by the rich tastes of the cream cheese, sour cream, and cheddar cheese."

In a roaster or large skillet, brown ground beef. Drain. Add seasonings, tomatoes, tomato sauce, and garlic; simmer 10 minutes.

Cook pasta as directed on package; drain. Add cream cheese and stir until cream cheese has melted. Add sour cream and green onions.

In a 9- x 13-inch (23 x 33 cm) buttered baking dish, layer the pasta, meat mixture and top with shredded cheese.

Bake covered at 325° (165° C) for 30 minutes. Uncover and bake another 15 minutes.

Baked Veal

2½ pounds (1 kg) veal

½ cup (70 g) flour

2 teaspoons paprika

2 teaspoons salt

1 teaspoon pepper

½ cup (115 g) butter

2 cloves garlic, minced

1½ cups (360 mL) water

1 beef bouillon cube

2 cups (480 g) sour cream

2 cups (300 g) sliced water chestnuts, drained

1 teaspoon basil

⅛ teaspoon rosemary

1 teaspoon lemon juice

¼ cup (60 mL) dry sherry

This casserole is loaded with good ingredients which makes this veal dish "top notch."

With a meat mallet, pound veal thin and cut into strips. Dip veal in a mixture of flour, paprika, salt, and pepper.

In a skillet, heat butter and garlic. Brown veal, adding more butter if necessary. Remove veal and garlic from skillet and discard garlic. Add water and bouillon cube and stir until dissolved.

Add sour cream, lower heat and mix thoroughly. Add veal, water chestnuts and remaining ingredients and stir. Pour into a sprayed, baking dish and bake at 350° (175° C) covered for 1 hour. Serve with rice.

Veal, Peppers, and Pasta

8-ounce (226 g) package linguine

1 pound (453 g) veal cutlets, sliced into strips

1 sweet red bell pepper, seeded, thinly sliced

8-ounce (226 g) package mushrooms, halved

½ cup (50 g) chopped celery

10-ounce (283 g) package frozen sweet peas

2 tablespoons butter

2 tablespoons flour

½ teaspoon seasoned salt

¼ teaspoon dried sweet basil

¼ teaspoon white pepper

¾ cup (180 mL) half-and-half cream

1 tablespoon capers, drained

Sweet red bell pepper and bright green peas make a colorful as well as a delicious casserole. The combination of ingredients in this dish gives it variety and substance, as well as flavor.

Cook linguine according to directions on package; drain. Butter a 9- x 13-inch (23 x 33 cm) baking dish and evenly spread linguine over the bottom of the dish.

Place veal strips over the linguine, overlapping if necessary. In a medium bowl, combine bell pepper, mushrooms, celery, and peas. Spoon over veal.

In a small saucepan, over medium heat, melt butter; mix in flour and seasonings. Gradually stir in cream.

Cook, stirring constantly until mixture has thickened. Pour sauce over veal and vegetables Bake covered at 350° (175° C) for 40 minutes.

Wonderful Ham Loaf

2 pounds (907 g) ground, cooked ham

½ pound (226 g) ground pork

⅔ cup (33 g) fresh breadcrumbs

½ cup (120 mL) whole milk

2 tablespoons brown sugar

¼ teaspoon celery salt

½ teaspoon black pepper

1 teaspoon dry mustard

1 tablespoon prepared horseradish

3 tablespoons finely minced green bell
pepper

2 eggs, slightly beaten

Mustard Sauce:

1 cup (240 mL) half-and-half cream

⅓ cup (60 g) packed light brown sugar

1 tablespoon dry mustard

1 tablespoon flour

Pinch of salt

1 egg yolk

½ cup (120 mL) vinegar

1 teaspoon minced dried parsley

You won't believe how good this is with the Mustard Sauce. The leftovers (if there are any) are just as good as the premier serving…cold or hot.

Combine the ground ham and ground pork well. (Your butcher can grind the two together or this is a good way to use left-over ham.)

Soak breadcrumbs in cream and add all remaining loaf ingredients together. Shape into a loaf on a greased 9- x 13-inch (23 x 33 cm) baking pan or line the pan with foil.

Bake at 350° (175° C) for 35 minutes; then turn oven down to 300° (150° C) and bake another 35 minutes. Let ham loaf cool for 5 to 10 minutes and carefully remove to a serving plate.

To make Mustard Sauce, place all ingredients in blender and process for about 20 seconds. Pour into a saucepan and cook until sauce is thickened. Serve warm.

Boeuf En Cocotte

3 to 3½ pounds (1.3 to 1.6 kg) rump or
    chuck roast or round steak

Seasoned salt

½ to 1 cup (50 to 100 g) flour

Oil

3 large white onions, sliced

2 bunches green onions and tops

Ground black pepper

10½-ounce (297 g) can beef broth

3 to 4 8-ounce (226 g) cans beer, not light

4 cloves garlic, finely minced

2 bay leaves

3 tablespoons chopped parsley

1 tablespoon brown sugar

1 tablespoon red wine vinegar

Beer is great for cooking lots of different foods and this dish proves it's great for beef. The malt in beer provides a slightly sweet quality and the hops balances the flavor with a slightly dry character.

Cut chuck roast in bite-size pieces, lay on paper towels and pat dry. Sprinkle with seasoned salt and dredge with flour. In a large skillet heat oil and brown each piece of beef on all sides. Add oil as needed. Drain beef on paper towels and set aside.

Chop green onions and tops into 1-inch (2.5-cm) pieces. Saute until transparent and tender and drain on paper towels. Place beef and onions in a baking dish and season with black ground pepper.

Add beef broth, 3 cans of beer, garlic, bay leaf and parsley. Stir to mix well. Cover and bake at 325° (165° C) for 1 hour. Remove from oven and make sure liquid is covering beef. Add more beer if necessary. (Beef should always be covered.)

Cover and cook for an additional 50 to 60 minutes or until beef is fork tender. Add brown sugar and vinegar to liquid, stir well and cook, covered, an additional 10 minutes. Remove bay leaves and garnish with parsley.

Seafood & Fish Casseroles

*F*ew meals are better than well-prepared seafood and fish, but as every seafood connoisseur knows, great recipes can be difficult to find. This chapter features an incredible variety of such recipes, from Seafood Baked Tomatoes (below), to a Swiss Crab Casserole (page 154), to a Crawfish Fettuccine (page 156). For special entertaining, try the Creole Chicken and Shrimp Casserole on page 160.

Seafood Baked Tomatoes

6 large, firm tomatoes

Salt

2 tablespoons butter

4 tablespoons minced green onions and tops

4 tablespoons minced celery

4 tablespoons minced green or red bell pepper

1½ tablespoons flour

1½ cups (360 mL) milk

1½ cups (600 g) crabmeat, chopped lobster or shrimp

2 teaspoons worcestershire sauce

½ teaspoon cayenne pepper

½ teaspoon salt

1 cup (100 g) grated cheddar cheese

Lettuce

Green onions with tops

Radishes

Celery with leaves

Parsley

Here's a quick casserole that looks stunning. Feel free to use canned crabmeat or shrimp if you don't have fresh on hand.

Hollow out tomatoes from stem end leaving enough meat to hold shape of tomato. Hollow out enough area to fill with seafood mixture for one serving. Lightly salt inside of tomatoes and invert on rack to drain for about 15 minutes.

In a skillet, melt butter and sauté onion, celery, and green pepper until tender and translucent. Stir in flour and whisk until smooth and all lumps are removed. Slowly stir in milk, stirring constantly.

Continue cooking and stirring until sauce has thickened to gravy consistency. Add seafood of choice and continue to stir. Add worcestershire, cayenne, salt, and cheese and stir until cheese has melted. Remove from heat.

Put tomato shells in baking dish, closed side down, and spoon in filling. Put baking dish in a roasting pan containing several inches of water and place in oven.

If tomatoes are ripe and shells don't hold their shape very well, put tomato shells in sprayed or well buttered muffin tins. Serve on a bed of lettuce and garnish with green onions, radishes, celery, and parsley.

Seafood Royale

1 cup (225 g) uncooked rice

2 10½-ounce cans cream of shrimp soup

¾ cup (180 mL) milk

⅔ cup (160 g) mayonnaise

½ teaspoon salt

¼ teaspoon white pepper

¼ teaspoon seasoned salt

½ teaspoon cayenne pepper

3 pounds (1.35 kg) cooked, peeled shrimp

6-ounce (170 g) can crabmeat, drained

1 onion, chopped

2 cups (200 g) chopped celery

4 tablespoons snipped parsley

5-ounce (141 g) can sliced water
    chestnuts, drained

Slivered almonds

A meal on the wharf! Just add hot buttered French bread and a green salad. (And maybe a bottle of white wine – no dessert needed!)

Cook rice according to package directions until fluffy. Whisk together soup, milk, and mayonnaise until smooth and creamy.

Add seasonings, shrimp, crabmeat, onion, celery, parsley, and water chestnuts. Stir in rice until well mixed. Add milk if dry.

Pour into sprayed 9- x 13-inch (23 x 33 cm) baking dish and sprinkle almonds over top. Bake at 350° (175° C) for 30 minutes or until heated thoroughly.

Swiss Crab Casserole

1 cup (230 g) butter, melted

3 cups (720 mL) milk

½ teaspoon white pepper

6 eggs

1 cup (150 g) biscuit mix

2 cups (220 g) grated Swiss cheese

2 cups (800 g) crabmeat

1 cup (240 g) mayonnaise

This hot crab dish can be served at luncheon or a brunch – and really sets off those taste buds.

Mix butter, milk, white pepper, eggs, and biscuit mix in blender until smooth. Pour into a sprayed 9- x 13-inch (23 x 33 cm) baking dish. Sprinkle with Swiss cheese.

In a bowl, mix crabmeat with mayonnaise and spread on top of cheese, gently pressing down into liquid. Bake at 350° (175° C) for 55 minutes. Remove from oven and let sit until firm.

Crab Casserole

½ cup (75 g) minced onion

¼ cup (50 g) minced celery

¼ cup (45 g) minced green bell pepper

1 clove garlic, minced

1 tablespoon chopped parsley

12 tablespoons butter, divided

2 cups (100 g) soft breadcrumbs, divided

½ cup (120 mL) cream

1 hard-boiled egg, chopped

1 tablespoon white wine vinegar

1 teaspoon worcestershire

¼ teaspoon thyme

1 teaspoon salt

Tabasco to taste

2 eggs, beaten

1 pound (453 g) crabmeat, washed, picked

Lemon

This crab casserole gives a luncheon a special touch when cooked in special pans known as ramekins. Ramekins are sometimes made of porcelain or earthenware and are shaped like a sea shell — they really dress up your salad plate.

In a skillet, saute vegetables in ¼ cup butter for 10 minutes or until tender. Add half of the breadcrumbs, cream, hard-boiled egg, and seasonings, mixing well. Add beaten eggs and crabmeat.

Melt remaining butter and mix with remaining bread-crumbs in separate bowl. Toss and reserve for topping. Pour crab mixture into individual ramekins. Top with buttered crumbs.

Bake in ¼-inch (6 mm) deep hot water bath for 10 minutes or until crumbs are golden. Serve with lemon.

Crabmeat Quiche

6-ounce (170 g) can crabmeat, drained

6 to 8 fresh mushrooms, sliced

⅔ cup (100 g) chopped green onion

½ cup (55 g) grated Swiss cheese

9-inch (23 cm) unbaked pie shell

2 eggs, beaten

½ cup (120 mL) milk

½ cup (120 g) mayonnaise

2 tablespoons flour

½ teaspoon salt

½ stick (60 g) butter, melted

Lunch or brunch – Crabmeat Quiche is a winner!

Flake crabmeat and remove shells. Combine crabmeat, mushrooms, green onion, and cheese, and place in pie shell.

Combine eggs, milk, mayonnaise, flour, salt, and beat well. Pour slowly over crabmeat. Add melted butter and bake at 350° (175° C) for 40 minutes.

Crawfish Fettuccine

12-ounce (340 g) package fettuccine

3 bell peppers, chopped

3 onions, chopped

5 ribs celery, chopped

3 sticks (345 g) butter

14-ounce (396 g) package frozen crawfish tails

2 tablespoons snipped parsley

3 to 4 cloves garlic, minced

1 pint (473 mL) half-and-half

½ cup (70 g) flour

1 pound (453 g) jalapeno cheese, cubed

This Crawfish Fettuccine will make you think you just flew into New Orleans.

Cook noodles according to directions. Drain and set aside. Saute bell pepper, onion, and celery in butter.

Add crawfish tails and simmer for 8 to 10 minutes, stirring occasionally. Add parsley, garlic and half-and-half and mix well. Gradually stir in flour, mixing well.

Simmer for 30 minutes, stirring occasionally. Add cheese and continue to stir until melted and blended. Mix fettuccine with sauce.

Pour all into sprayed 6-quart (6.5 L) baking dish. Bake at 300° (150° C) for 15 to 20 minute or until heated throughout.

Snow Pea Shrimp

3 cups (300 g) penne pasta

½ cup (115 g) butter

3 cloves garlic, minced

2 green onions, minced

2 cups (150 g) sliced fresh mushrooms

½ cup (70 g) flour

½ teaspoon salt

½ teaspoon pepper

15-ounce (425 g) can chicken broth

2 cups (480 mL) milk

3 tablespoons dry white wine

¾ cup (80 g) grated Swiss cheese

2¼ cups (250 g) frozen snow peas, thawed and drained

1 pound (453 g) fresh shrimp, cleaned, cooked, peeled

½ cup (40 g) grated parmesan cheese

¼ to ½ cup (20 to 40 g) sliced almonds

With pasta, shrimp, snow peas, and cheese, you can't go wrong.

Cook and drain pasta according to package directions. In a large deep skillet, melt butter and sauté garlic, onion, and mushrooms over low heat. Continue cooking until mushrooms are tender; stir occasionally.

Add flour, salt and pepper stirring constantly over medium heat. Stir until all lumps are out and sauce is smooth and bubbly. Gradually stir in broth, milk, and wine and stir continuously until smooth.

Turn to high heat, bring to boiling, and stir in Swiss cheese. Stir until cheese is melted and remove from heat. Add snow peas, shrimp, and pasta to mushroom mixture and stir to mix well.

Pour into sprayed 9- x 13-inch (23 x 33 cm) baking dish. Sprinkle parmesan and almonds over top. Bake at 350° (175° C) for 20 to 25 minutes or until golden brown on top.

Shrimp and Wild Rice En Cocotte

1 cup (225 g) wild rice

5¼ cups (1.2 L) chicken stock, divided

1 onion, chopped

1 pound (453 g) mushrooms, sliced

1 clove garlic, minced

¼ cup (60 g) butter

2 tablespoons flour

½ cup (120 mL) dry white wine

¼ teaspoon salt

¼ teaspoon pepper

1 teaspoon tarragon, crushed

1½ pounds (680 g) cooked shrimp, shelled, veined

Here's a shrimp dish that "takes the cake!"

Place rice and 4 cups stock in saucepan. Bring to boil. Simmer, covered 45-50 minutes. Uncover. Fluff with fork. Simmer 5 minutes. Pour off any excess stock.

Saute onion, mushrooms, and garlic in butter 5 minutes. Add flour. Stir over medium heat 3 minutes. Add remaining stock and wine. Stir until slightly thickened. Add salt, pepper and tarragon.

Combine rice-mushroom mixture and shrimp. Pour into sprayed 2-quart (2 L) casserole. Bake covered at 350° (175° C) for 30 minutes.

Creole Chicken and Shrimp

1 tablespoon pickling spice

1½ pounds shrimp, peeled, veined

4 tablespoons olive oil

4 boneless, skinless chicken breast halves

1 bunch green onions and tops, chopped

½ cup chopped celery

⅓ cup chopped red bell pepper

⅓ cup chopped green bell pepper

8-ounce can tomato sauce

½ cup white wine

¼ teaspoon Tabasco sauce

1 tablespoon worcestershire sauce

2 to 3 tablespoons snipped parsley

¼ teaspoon thyme

1½ teaspoons salt

½ teaspoon pepper

1 cup half-and-half cream

Rice

The best of the culinary world!

Fill large pot ¾ full with water and bring to a boil. Add pickling spice and shrimp and cook until shrimp turn pink. Remove shrimp, drain and chill.

In large skillet, heat oil and brown chicken on both sides and saute until centers are no longer pink. Remove from skillet and drain on paper towel. Cool and cut into bite-size pieces.

Put onion, celery, and peppers in the skillet and saute until onion is translucent. Add chicken to skillet and stir in tomato sauce, white wine, Tabasco, worcestershire sauce, parsley, thyme, salt, and pepper, and mix well.

Pour into a 4-quart (4.5 L) baking dish and bake at 350° (175° C) for 40 to 45 minutes. Remove chicken dish and stir in shrimp and half-and-half. Bake until heated throughout. Serve over rice.

Sun-Dried Tomatoes and Shrimp

1 pound (453 g) shrimp, cleaned

1 tablespoon pickling spice

½ teaspoon salt

1 pound (453 g) spaghetti

1½ cups (340 g) small curd cottage cheese, drained

12-ounce (340 g) can evaporated milk

2 cloves garlic, minced

½ teaspoon salt

½ teaspoon white pepper

¼ teaspoon red pepper flakes

2 tablespoons extra-virgin olive oil

1 cup (150 g) sun-dried tomatoes, chopped

4 ounces (113 g) feta cheese

1 cup (60 g) chopped fresh basil leaves

¼ cup (15 g) chopped fresh parsley

This casserrole features superb flavor and shrimp at its finest!

In large pot, cover shrimp with water, season with pickling spice and bring to a boil. Cook until shrimp is pink.

Remove shrimp from water and drain. Set aside. Rinse pot and fill with water. Bring to boil, add salt and spaghetti. Cook spaghetti until al dente, drain and set aside.

In a blender, combine cottage cheese, evaporated milk, garlic, salt, pepper, red pepper, and process on high until well blended. Continue processing on high and slowly pour oil in blender until well blended.

Pour into large saucepan and cook on low heat, stirring constantly. Do not boil. Slowly add shrimp, continue stirring until slightly thickened. Remove from heat.

Put spaghetti in serving bowl and pour sauce-shrimp mixture over spaghetti. Toss to mix. Add sun-dried tomatoes, feta cheese, and basil and toss again. Garnish with fresh parsley.

Shrimp Tetrazzini

1 stick (115 g) butter, divided

4 green onions with tops, chopped

1 cup (240 mL) water

5 tablespoons flour

2½ cups (600 mL) chicken broth

½ cup (120 m L) clam juice

½ cup (120 mL) white wine

½ cup (120 mL) cooking sherry

½ cup (120 mL) cream

½ teaspoon oregano

1 cup (85 g) grated parmesan cheese

This is not your ordinary Tetrazzini — shrimp makes it "top notch" and company fare.

In skillet, melt half the butter. Add green onions and water and bring to a boil. Reduce heat and simmer until water has boiled away and only the butter remains and onions are soft.

Stir in flour until smooth and cook for about 3 minutes. Do not brown. Add broth, clam juice, wine, sherry, cream, and oregano. Cook, stirring constantly with a whisk, until sauce begins to boil. Stir in cheese and set aside.

Melt remaining butter with oil over high heat. Saute

2 tablespoons oil

1 pound (453 g) mushrooms, sliced

½ teaspoon garlic salt

8 ounces (226 g) spaghetti

2 pounds (907 g) shrimp, cooked, shelled, veined

½ teaspoon salt

¼ teaspoon pepper

Grated parmesan cheese

mushrooms and garlic salt until brown, about 4 minutes. Cook spaghetti according to package directions; drain. Mix everything with shrimp and season with salt and pepper. Pour into a 3-quart (3 L) baking dish and top with parmesan cheese. Bake uncovered at 375° (190° C) for 15 to 20 minutes or until saucy bubbles and is brown.

Cheesy Shrimp Casserole

8-ounce (226 g) package angel hair pasta

8-ounce (226 g) package shredded Swiss cheese

8-ounce (226 g) package feta cheese, crumbled

8-ounce (226 g) carton plain yogurt

1 cup (240 mL) evaporated milk

4 eggs

½ cup (50 g) fresh parsley, snipped

1 teaspoon basil

1 teaspoon oregano

3 cloves garlic, minced

16-ounce (453 g) jar chunky salsa

1 pound (453 g) uncooked shrimp, peeled, deveined

16-ounce (453 g) package grated mozzarella cheese

Wow! These three cheeses and the salsa make this shrimp dish a 10!

Cook pasta according to directions on package, drain and set aside. Preheat oven to 350° (175° C).

In large mixing bowl, combine the Swiss and feta cheeses, yogurt, milk, eggs, parsley, basil, oregano, and garlic.

In a sprayed 9- x 13-inch (23 x 33 cm) baking dish, spread half the pasta, half the cheese mixture, half the salsa and half shrimp in layers. Repeat layers using all remaining pasta, cheese mixture, salsa and shrimp.

Sprinkle top with mozzarella and bake 350° (175° C) for 30 to 40 minutes or until heated throughout. Cool slightly before serving.

Shrimp Strata

5 slices white bread

Butter, softened

10 to 12 ounces (283 to 340 g) fresh shrimp, cooked, cut in bite-size pieces

8-ounce (226 g) package shredded cheddar cheese

2 tablespoons dried flaked onions

3 eggs, beaten

1½ cups (360 mL) half-and-half cream

½ teaspoon seasoned salt

¼ teaspoon white pepper

1 teaspoon dry mustard

Paprika

Leftover ham can be substituted for the shrimp.

Spread the softened butter over the 5 slices of white bread. Cut into 1-inch (2.5 cm) cubes.

Butter a 9- x 13-inch (23 x 33 cm) baking dish and place half the bread cubes over bottom of dish. Layer half the shrimp and cheese. Make one more layer of the bread cubes, shrimp, and cheese, then sprinkle flaked onions over top.

In a bowl, combine the eggs, half-and-half, salt, pepper, and mustard; mix well. Pour over layered mixture.

Cover and let set in refrigerator overnight or at least 4 to 5 hours. Bake uncovered at 325° (165° C) for 45 minutes. Cool for 5 to 10 minutes before serving.

Fresh Shrimp Pasta Bake

2 pounds (907 g) shrimp, shelled, veined

½ cup (115 g) butter

8-ounce (226 g) package spinach linguine

1 cup (242 g) sour cream

1 cup (242 g) mayonnaise

10½ ounce (297 g) cream of mushroom soup

1 teaspoon dijon mustard

¼ cup (60 mL) dry sherry

1 tablespoons minced fresh chives

¾ cup (75 g)shredded sharp cheddar cheese

The richness of this pasta dish gives a creamy, delightful taste that blends well with shrimp.

In large skillet, saute shrimp in butter for 3 to 5 minutes, stirring often. Remove from heat and set aside.

Cook pasta al dente according to package directions. Drain and place evenly in sprayed 9- x 13-inch (23 x 33 cm) baking dish. Pour shrimp over pasta and spread out in a second layer.

In a separate bowl, combine sour cream, mayonnaise, mushroom soup, mustard, sherry, and chives. Mix thoroughly and pour over shrimp and pasta.

Spread cheese on top of mixture and bake at 350° (175° C) for 30 minutes.

Shrimp and Artichokes

1 onion, chopped

3 ribs of celery, chopped

2 cloves garlic, finely minced

2 sweet red bell peppers, chopped

1 green bell pepper

⅔ stick (80 g) butter

3 pounds (1.4 kg) shrimp, boiled, peeled, and deveined

3½ cups (875 g) cooked white rice

½ cup (120 mL) tomato sauce

8-ounce (240 mL) carton whipping cream

½ to ¾ teaspoon red pepper

½ teaspoon seasoned salt

2 14-ounce (397 g) cans artichoke hearts, drained, halved

2 cups (200 g) shredded cheddar cheese

To make this casserole ahead of time, cover before you sprinkle on cheese and refrigerate until ready to bake. Sprinkle on cheese just before baking.

In a large skillet, saute onion, celery, garlic, and bell peppers in the butter. Add cooked shrimp and rice, mixing well. Add tomato sauce, cream, red pepper, salt, and artichoke hearts, mix well.

Pour into a buttered 9- x 13-inch (23 x 33 cm) baking dish. Sprinkle with cheese and bake at 350° (175° C) for 30 minutes or until ingredients are thoroughly heated.

Baked Shrimp Gratinee

½ cup (115 g) butter, softened

3 teaspoons garlic salt, divided

2½ to 3 pounds (1.1 to 1.3 kg) cooked shrimp, shelled, veined

1 cup (100 g) grated parmesan cheese, divided

1 quart (900 g) small curd cottage cheese, undrained

1 cup (100 g) cracker crumbs

1½ cups (112 g) slivered almonds, toasted

¼ cup (60 g) butter, sliced

Gratinee refers to dishes topped with cheese, breadcrumbs, and butter slices and heated. This delectable dish qualifies on all counts.

Spread butter mixed with 1 teaspoon garlic salt over sides and bottom of 3-quart (3 L) baking dish. Spread layer of shrimp on bottom and sprinkle with 1 teaspoon garlic salt and ½ cup parmesan cheese.

Make a second layer of cottage cheese on top of shrimp and again sprinkle with 1 teaspoon garlic salt and remaining parmesan cheese.

Top with cracker crumbs, then butter slices and finally almonds. Bake at 350° (175° C) for 25 to 30 minutes.

Shrimp Feta Flambe

1 white onion, chopped

2 ribs celery, sliced

½ cup (120 mL) olive oil

15-ounce (425 g) can diced tomatoes

4-ounce (113 g) can chopped green chiles

2 tablespoons chopped, fresh cilantro

½ teaspoon seasoned salt

¼ teaspoon cayenne pepper

2 cloves garlic, minced

2½ pounds (1.1 kg) shrimp, lightly cooked, peeled, and deveined

½ pound (226 g) feta cheese

¼ cup (60 mL) vodka

Hot cooked white rice

This dramatic presentation will impress the most sophisticated of guests, even if the flame is a small one. The higher the alcohol content of the liquor added, the higher the flame.

In a large saucepan, saute onion and celery in oil until transparent. Add tomatoes, green chiles, cilantro, salt, pepper, and garlic. Cover and simmer for 45 minutes.

Add shrimp to sauce and spoon into a buttered 3-quart (3 L) baking dish. Crumble cheese over shrimp.

Bake uncovered at 350° (175° C) for 10 to 15 minutes. Remove from oven. When ready to serve, pour heated vodka over shrimp and flame. Serve over hot white rice.

Crackered Oysters

2 pints (1 L) fresh oysters

2 tablespoons lemon juices

½ cup (115 g) melted butter

2 cups (350 g) crumbled saltine crackers, divided

Cracked black pepper

½ pint half-and-half cream

½ teaspoon worcestershire sauce

½ teaspoon salt

2 teaspoons dry white wine

Oyster lovers – come and get it!

Drain oysters and reserve liquid. Combine lemon juice and melted butter and stir to mix. Pour over cracker crumbs, stir and toss to mix.

In a sprayed 9- x 13-inch (23 x 33 cm) baking dish, spread one-third of the cracker crumbs over bottom of dish. Layer half the oysters and repeat with another third of the cracker crumbs and remaining oysters.

Lightly grind cracked black pepper over oysters. Mix together reserved oyster liquid and enough half-and-half to equal one cup.

Stir in worcestershire, salt and wine. Pour over oysters and sprinkle remaining cracker crumbs over top.

Bake at 350° (175° C) for 30 minutes or until well heated.

Corn-Oyster Casserole

1 quart (1 L) oysters, drained, quartered

2 15-ounce (849 g) cans cream-style corn

½ cup (120 mL) evaporated milk

1 teaspoon salt

½ teaspoon pepper

⅛ teaspoon Tabasco sauce

3 cups (525 g) crumbled saltine crackers

1 cup (230 g) butter, melted

Invite the neighbors for a Saturday night supper. This casserole is easy to make and will be a surprising new dish!

In a bowl mix oysters with corn, milk, salt, pepper, and Tabasco. Add crackers to melted butter and put in a sprayed baking dish. Top with oyster mixture. Bake at 350° (175° C) for 40 minutes.

Baked Oysters Creole

1 cup (240 g) butter

1¼ cups (125 g) minced celery

1 green or red bell pepper, diced

1 bunch fresh green onions with tops, diced

3 cloves garlic, minced

1 cup (240 mL) whipping cream

2 pints (1 L) oysters in liquid

1 tablespoon hot sauce

2 tablespoons worcestershire sauce

1 teaspoon salt

3 eggs, hardboiled, chopped

3 cups (270 g) seasoned dry breadcrumbs

1 teaspoon salt

Celery, bell pepper, green onions, and garlic are staples in Louisiana dishes and this recipe is no exception. Similar to a stuffing, this oyster dish can be served as a casserole side dish any time of day.

In a heavy saucepan, melt butter over moderate heat and saute celery, bell pepper, onion, and garlic several minutes until all appear translucent and tender.

Slowly pour in whipping cream, stirring constantly and bring to almost boiling and reduce heat. Continue stirring and add oysters with its liquid and cook until oysters have curled.

Remove from heat and add hot sauce, worcestershire, salt, and eggs. Stir in 1 cup (90 g) breadcrumbs and stir. Continue adding breadcrumbs and stir until consistency is moist, but firm enough to hold its shape.

Spoon into sprayed 9- x 13-inch (23 x 33 cm) baking dish and bake at 350° (175°) for 50 to 60 minutes.

Georgia Oyster Casserole

2 quarts (2 L) oysters

1 stick (120 g) butter, divided

4 whole scallions, chopped

1 cup (180 g) chopped green or red bell
  pepper

1½ (110 g) cups sliced mushrooms

¼ cup (35 g) flour

1 cup (240 mL) whipping cream

⅓ cup (35 g) grated parmesan cheese

Freshly grated nutmeg

½ teaspoon paprika

Salt to taste

Freshly ground black pepper

¾ cup (70 g) breadcrumbs

Maybe you'll find a pearl!

Drain the oysters and set aside. In a large skillet melt 2 tablespoons butter. Add scallions and bell pepper and saute until the vegetables are tender. Add mushrooms and oysters and saute for 5 minutes.

In a separate pan, melt 2 tablespoons of the remaining butter over medium low heat. Add flour, stirring constantly until smooth. Add the cream and stir constantly until bubbling and thick.

Mix in cheese, then pour cheese sauce into the oyster mixture and season with nutmeg, paprika, salt and pepper. Let simmer 3 to 5 minutes.

Pour the mixture into sprayed 9- x 13-inch (23 x 33 cm) baking dish and top with breadcrumbs and dot with the remaining butter. Place under the broiler until browned and bubbling, about 10 minutes.

Flounder and Spinach Bake

2 10-ounce (283 g) packages frozen chopped spinach

8-ounce (225 g) carton sour cream

½ onion, finely chopped

½ sweet red bell pepper, chopped

2 tablespoons flour

2 tablespoons lemon juice

1 tablespoon cream

¾ teaspoon seasoned salt

¼ teaspoon pepper

6 to 8 flounder fillets

⅔ cup (50 g) fresh sliced mushrooms

Paprika

The fresh taste of flounder is enhanced by spinach and mushrooms, and serving it on a bed of spinach sets off the as the delicate feast it is.

Cook spinach according to package directions. Drain very well. In a bowl, combine sour cream, onion, bell pepper, flour, lemon juice, cream, and seasoned salt, mixing well.

Add half of the mixture to the spinach, mixing well. Place spinach mixture in a 9- x 13-inch (23 x 33 cm) buttered baking dish. Arrange flounder on top of spinach. Place mushrooms around flounder.

Top with remaining sour cream mixture and sprinkle with paprika. Bake at 375° (190° C) for 15 to 20 minutes or until fish flakes easily.

Sole with Mornay Sauce

6 to 8 filets of sole

Salt

Pepper

White wine

½ stick (60 g) butter

¼ cup (25 g) flour

2 cups (480 mL) half-and-half cream

1 cup (100 g) grated swiss cheese

Grated parmesan cheese

This is an exceptional dish for any full-flavored seafood. With all its rich and creamy texture, select a fish that can stand up to this special sauce.

Place sole in a large skillet. Sprinkle with salt and pepper; pour in enough white wine to just barely cover fish. Cook until fish flakes easily when tested with fork.

Carefully remove fish to a shallow baking dish and keep warm. In a saucepan, melt butter and add flour, stirring well. Add cream to the butterand flour mixture, stirring well.

Cook (do not boil), stirring vigorously, until sauce is smooth and creamy. Remove sauce from heat and let cool several minutes. Stir in the Swiss cheese.

Pour sauce over fish and sprinkle with parmesan cheese. Place in a very hot oven (about 425° F, (215° C) and bake about 10 minutes or until cheese begins to glaze.

Seafood Medley Casserole

1 pound (453 g) crabmeat

1 pound (453 g) scallops

1 pound (453 g) shrimp, shelled, veined

6 eggs, hardboiled, chopped

2 cups (480 mL) whipping cream

¾ cup (75 g) shredded swiss cheese

2 tablespoons flour

1 teaspoon dry mustard

1 teaspoon alt

1 teaspoon white pepper

⅓ to ½ cup (80 to 120 mL) milk (optional)

2 1-pound (453 g) packages fettuccine,
    linguine, or pappardelle pasta

Fresh crabmeat, scallops, and shrimp are good anytime, but when served over your favorite ribbon pastas they become a special treat for special occasions.

In a sprayed 9- x 13-inch (23 x 33 cm) baking dish, place uncooked crabmeat, scallops, and shrimp. Sprinkle chopped egg on top of seafood and set aside.

In a heavy saucepan over moderate heat, heat cream almost to boiling. Remove from heat and stir in Swiss cheese. Continue to stir until cheese melts.

In a separate dish, mix together flour, mustard, salt, and pepper and pour into cream and cheese mixture. As sauce is stirred it will thicken slightly. If sauce thickens beyond a thin sauce then add up to ½ cup milk to thin.

Pour sauce over seafood and bake at 350° (175° C) for 30 to 35 minutes. Serve over fettuccine, linguine, pappardelle, tagliarini, or tagliatelle pasta cooked al dente as package directs.

Acknowledgments

Many people deserve thanks for their contributions to this book.

Artists whose pottery is featured in the photographs — Adrienne Dellinger (Pots with Purpose, Charlotte, NC), Sue Hintz (Salvatorra Potter, Weaverville, NC), and Nick Joerling (Penland, North Carolina);

Friends and colleagues for trusting us with their treasured casserole dishes — Greg Evans, Tracy Hildebrand, Dana Irwin, Marthe Le Van, Susan McBride, Celia Naranjo, and Rob Pulleyn;

Chris Bryant and Skip Wade for use of their home;

Robin Dimsdle at Cookbook Resources for her patience and overall helpfulness;

and the creative team whose energy and talent contributed to the visual appeal of this book: photographer Evan Bracken, art director Megan Kirby, and chefs David Rowland and Scott Schronce.